清末西人在華企業

WESTERN ENTERPRISE IN LATE CH'ING CHINA

A Selective Survey of Jardine, Matheson & Company's Operations, 1842-1895

Edward LeFevour

D1636649

Harvard East Asian Monographs

LIBRARY
WISCONSIN STATE UNIVERSITY
Stevens Point, Wis. 54481

HARVARD EAST ASIAN MONOGRAPHS

26

WESTERN ENTERPRISE IN LATE CH'ING CHINA
A SELECTIVE SURVEY OF JARDINE,
MATHESON AND COMPANY'S OPERATIONS

1842–1895

WESTERN ENTERPRISE IN LATE CH'ING CHINA
A SELECTIVE SURVEY OF JARDINE,
MATHESON AND COMPANY'S OPERATIONS
1842 - 1895

by

Edward Le Fevour

Published by
East Asian Research Center
Harvard University

Distributed by
Harvard University Press
Cambridge, Mass.
1968

HF
3776
.L35

Copright, 1968, by

the President and Fellows of

Harvard University

The East Asian Research Center at Harvard
University administers research projects
designed to further scholarly understanding
of China, Korea, Japan, and adjacent areas.
These studies have been assisted by grants
from the Ford Foundation.

LIBRARY
WISCONSIN STATE UNIVERSITY
Stevens Point, Wis. 54481

ACKNOWLEDGEMENTS

This volume is a revision of a doctoral dissertation completed at Peterhouse, Cambridge University, almost ten years ago. I am indebted to my research supervisor, Professor M.M. Postan, for direction and unfailing kindness. I thank Jardine, Matheson and Co. for permitting access to the archive and owe a special debt to Norah Bartlett, its cataloguer. I thank the East Asian Research Center, Harvard, for financial aid and Professor John K. Fairbank for steady encouragement. I am grateful to Professor Jerry S. Clegg, to Olive Holmes for editorial assistance, and I thank my wife, Julia.

Berkeley, California   Edward LeFevour
1968

v

150887

150587

CONTENTS

INTRODUCTION

China's foreign trade in the latter half of the nineteenth century has been most often described in bold outline, though some historians have dealt with special areas in more detail.[1] The basic features of the trade were the relative smallness of total annual values, a tendency to prolonged stagnation, the dominance of a few commodities (tea and silk among exports, opium and cotton goods among imports), and the concentration of import growth in the final decade of the period. It is also clear that foreign trade meant little to the economy of China in aggregate terms and was insignificant in relation to China's population and the assumed vast internal trade.[2] Its most important feature was the absence of an encouraging demand for any of the products offered by the West, except Indian opium, until the rise in demand for cotton goods toward the end of the period.

We now understand that the probable causes of China's long resistance to foreign products were the self-sufficient nature of the traditional economy, poor communications, inland taxes such as likin, and worsening poverty throughout the century.[3] But in our present state of knowledge we cannot be certain about the relative importance of these causes. We know even less about the economic effects in China of strong Western demand for China's tea and silk or of the effects of opium import. Undoubtedly Western demand for these pruducts contributed to a rise in per capita product in some areas, since consular reports refer to the amazing absorption of silver sycee in exchange for tea and silk[4] and the opium trade is credited with causing or at least aggravating the inflation of the 1830's.[5] Beyond such general influences, there is no certain knowledge of the effect of foreign trade upon the domestic economy of nineteenth-century China.

The only measurable result was the creation of the treaty ports whose self-generating economic growth constituted a true leading sector which could have initiated fundamental and favorable changes in the traditional economy if the Ch'ing bureaucracy had cooperated. As it was, large Western firms found their commercial energies largely confined to the treaty ports, where and from which they struggled to change the economic thinking and the investment policies of Chinese merchants and officials.

The purpose of this study, therefore, is to examine aspects of Western entrepreneurial behavior and its effects in late Ch'ing China (the period between the treaty of Nanking and the Sino-Japanese war, 1842-1895) from the surviving records of the largest Western firm in China during those years, Jardine, Matheson and Company. This firm's "country trade" ancestry and founding have been explained by Michael Greenberg in his British Trade and the Opening of China, 1800-1842. After 1842 the firm's records expand so greatly that one must choose points of reference in order to control the material. In preparing this study I have limited myself, therefore, to an attempt to explore, as explicitly as the materials would allow, first, how an enterprising nineteenth-century Western firm acted in an environment alien and even hostile to such a business organization, second, what this firm's conception of its own role in China was (that is, to ask whether the pursuit of profit maximization necessarily made the firm imperialistic), and, finally, to explore the way in which the interaction between this single large firm and the bureaucracy influenced modernization efforts in late Ch'ing China.

This book, then, is not a history of the firm. A business history, concentrating upon organization, control, and management cannot be written from these records alone, since the activities of the firm as a profit-making unit will not be understood without reference to the records for the period of Matheson and Company, their London associate; these records have been destroyed.[6] So many of the administrative decisions made by Jardine, Matheson and Company were obviously influenced by the London firm, whose head was often the retired senior partner of the China firm, that it is hardly possible to mark out a clear path of the development of the China House without reference to Matheson and Company's records.[7] From the Jardine records, only, it has been possible to indicate how the firm in China adapted itself to the special circumstances of trade in China, including those which had ruined competitors, to outline the firm's development as an agency house, its commission business in trade and the service of trade, and its business as merchant investor, against the background of China's economic and political decay. However, the great size of the archive and my own training required a limited study. I have not attempted economic analysis because the quantitative data is lacking or discontinuous; very important subjects, such as shipping enterprise, export agency, and business in Japan, also are deliberately excluded.

On the basis of what I found and understood in the archive, I hope to show that Western firms in nineteenth-century China pursued policies which could have laid the foundation for economic modernization in a less resistant social-political context. In fact, Jardine's experience shows how Western enterprise reacted to this context and was compelled to modify normal business practice by the nature of Chinese society and the condition of the Chinese economy during the last century.

I also hope to show that Jardine, Matheson and Company did not consistently favor the "forward policy" of applying political and military pressure to a recalcitrant Chinese government. Their role in China, as senior members of the firm saw it, was closer to current concepts of technical and financial aid for economic development than to late nineteenth-century concepts of economic imperialism.

Finally, the firm's records provide a limited view of the social as well as the economic interaction of Chinese and Westerners, the mutual cooperation of merchants in the dominant opium trade and later in a wide range of joint investment, the relations between Ch'ing officials and members of the firm, and the firm's response to these relations. A close reading of such interaction indicates the historical complexity behind the phrase "Western impact," assumed by many to have been deliberately aggressive in all its manifestations.[8]

The correspondence shows that the traditional order was not defenseless against the offers of loans or of railroads, that officials were capable of balancing one large Western firm against another in competitive business just as they later managed, for a time, to balance foreign powers in China, and that this large Western firm was not as aggressive in dealing with Ch'ing officials as internal conditions would have allowed. In the final quarter of the century, Jardine, Matheson and Company aimed to achieve a position of influence within the traditional Chinese social order without necessarily weakening it. Though the firm's financial superiority rested upon treaty rights taken by force, its partners believed that progress in China, after 1870, depended upon cooperation with the bureaucracy. This does not deny that Jardine's activity was an important part of a larger process in which the entire traditional order suffered a collapse undoubtedly accelerated by Western economic, military, and political presnece in nineteenth-century China.

Thus my general intention has been to describe Jardine, Matheson and Company as a significant example of an adaptable profit-making unit mediating foreign trade with China, and to show something of how this unit acted upon and reacted to Chinese society in the last century.

Chapter I

THE OPIUM TRADE

Opium consumption in China became a matter of grave concern to the Ch'ing government in the late 1830's. The private "country traders" at Canton eroded, then supplanted, the East India Company's monopoly and within six years (1834-1840) expanded trade in opium so rapidly that the consequent outflow of silver bullion alarmed the mercantilists within the Chinese government. The drain of silver to India was believed to be causing a depreciation of copper cash, the ordinary medium for payment of land taxes, against silver; commodity prices were rising in many provinces and discontent increased proportionately.[1] The annual export of perhaps ten million dollars in silver in 1839 finally brought the imperial government to the decisive action of appointing Lin Tse-hsü commissioner.[2] War followed.

The Opium War was an attempt by both the Chinese and the British to settle the problems of diplomatic and commercial intercourse which grew out of the replacement of East India Company authority by that of the British government in China, and out of the burgeoning opium traffic. Commissioner Lin and the imperial government sought to preserve the framework of tribute by destroying a disruptive illegal trade and disciplining the "barbarians"; British authority seized upon the Chinese action as an opportunity to settle the matter by force on Western terms.

Upon signing the Treaty of Nanking and the supplementary treaties, China entered the comity of Western nations. Among the provisions setting forth the legal basis of the new system

in which Chinese diplomatic and commercial rights were de-
lineated, there is no mention of opium.[3] There were two
reasons for this omission: Chinese refusal to countenance
legalization and British refusal to discontinue production
in India. A study of the diplomatic records shows how much
more complex the framework of foreign trade had become with
the initiation of the treaty era.[4] A new relationship had
developed, closer to the Chinese economic and political order,
to replace the relatively simple one of Cohong, country trader,
and the East India Company Select Committee.

But the character of pre-treaty trade carried over
into the new era. The overwhelming dominance of tea among
exports (silk via Shanghai became important after 1845), and
of opium among imports, continued through the next quarter
century. Opium remained the most profitable trade commodity
for decades.

The social disorder which had probably first stimulated
demand increased rapidly after the war. In 1845 the annual
value of opium imported was estimated to have been twenty-five
to thirty million dollars for some years past and in that
year the trade probably put China £2,000,000 into debt.[5] The
auditor-general of the new colony of Hong Kong reported to the
governor in November of that year that there were eighty
clippers engaged in carrying opium to and from Hong Kong,
nineteen of which were registered to Jardine, Matheson and
Company.[6] Jardine's correspondence often contained remarks
such as "this year will long be remembered in China for the
depression which has existed in trade, with the single ex-
ception of opium."[7] While other imports stagnated from 1846,
opium imports grew so rapidly that illegal trade dominated
all foreign trade during the interwar decade, as it had prior

to 1842,[8] and all authorities agree that the drug was the most important item among China's imports until the final decade of the century.[9]

Jardine, Matheson and Company's continued investment in the trade was inevitable. Profit from opium had given the firm a commanding lead as agent and merchant in both export from India and import to China, and its coastal distribution system, based upon a large shipping fleet, ensured that this lead would be held whether opium imports were legalized or not.[10] The firm favored the "opening of China" to other goods but, from 1846, in common with the entire foreign merchant community, it attributed lack of demand for manufactured goods to Chinese taxes along the inland trade routes and to the heavy tax on tea in England which restricted demand for China's major export.[11] Thus the firm's assessment of Chinese markets through the late forties and the fifties encouraged continued investment in Indian opium and toleration of poorly-selling British exports. This continued basic reliance upon opium required close links with India houses, in the tradition of the old China trade, but it also required a more elaborate and expensive distribution and sales system in China as new centers began to develop. The evolution of this system through two decades further tied the firm to opium. It also brought the firm into daily contact with large numbers of Chinese employees, merchants, and officials who provided the market information and the smuggling facilities which made the trade possible.

Good profits, an early lead, and rising demand, then, explain Jardine, Matheson Company's continued investment in the opium business. The conclusions reached in the report of the Select Committee of the House of Commons (1847) were not relevant to this growing trade. In attributing poor markets

for British manufactured goods in China to the restricted
purchasing power of the Chinese people and in suggesting
increased British consumption of Chinese products as an
effective remedy[12] the committee avoided the question of what
the effects of large and increasing opium imports upon Chinese
purchasing power would be. Since 1843, and especially after
1845 and the collapse of the market for British manufactures
in China, many businessmen in Britain and China blamed opium
for absorbing the purchasing power of the Chinese to the de-
triment of all other imports. They maintained that British
piece goods required a certain level of circulation within
China in order to impress buyers and initiate a growing demand,
as in India. Chinese dealers, they argued, were concerned with
opium and the exchange of tea capital against it, not with
giving manufactured goods sufficient vent; therefore Anglo-
Indian opium firms were retarding home productivity and preventing the opening of a vast market for piece goods.[13]

Complaints about the opium trade in British manufacturing centers through the forties and fifties were especially
loud in 1854 when exports of cotton piece goods and woolens
to China totaled less in value and volume than they had eight
years previously.[14] Much of the complaint was specifically
directed against Jardine's as the leading opium firm; therefore a public defense was made to justify the company's expansion in opium:

> Instead of tending to restrict what is called the
> legitimate trade, the traffic in Opium has enormously
> extended the export of tea and silk from China to the
> British market, and enabled these articles to be
> supplied to consumers at a lower price than could
> otherwise have been the case. Indeed, but for it,

they could not have been shipped but for a limited extent
during the past two years, owing to the absolute want of
the means to pay for them. Being ourselves large importers
of British manufactures into China, nothing would afford
us greater satisfaction than to see this branch of trade
extended, but the demand for such goods is dependent upon
other considerations and it is in no way affected by the
Opium Trade.[15]

In arguing that profit from opium was the catalyst of
China's foreign trade in this period, the firm was certainly
correct; British demand for Chinese products could not have
become much more dependent upon the export of silver from Europe.
Anglo-Chinese trade had persisted in the triangular pattern
established during the 1830's, but within the "trilateral circuit"
changes followed upon the increased volume of exports and the
continued expansion of the opium trade. Shipments of silver and
gold bullion flowed into the hands of Chinese exporters of tea
and silk from 1848-1850 until the early sixties because the
demand for opium in China did not keep pace with the European
demand for tea and silk. In 1846 Alexander Matheson had written
that "there is a scarcity of money in China as in England and
India, $21,000,000 in Sycee have been taken from China to
England in the last three years."[16] However, by 1849, bullion
exports to England stopped as silk exports from Shanghai grew
in volume beyond all expectations and tea shipments were also
increasing. In the next year small shipments of silver bullion
began to arrive from England; these became larger and more regular during 1852-1853. In 1854 the firm warned its correspondents
of the continued balance in China's favor:

> While business in imports continues so restricted as
> of late...the Balance of Trade will be against us to the
> extent of three to four million pounds of sterling.
> This deficit requires to be provided for by an importation
> of Bullion which we may have difficulty in getting if war
> (with Russia) breaks out in Europe. Try to lay down funds
> in Spanish dollars.[17]

Further correspondence through the decade reported the arrival
of several steamers with cargoes of bullion from Europe, one
carrying £700,000 on a single voyage.[18] Silver bullion (estimated
at one to two million pounds per year)[19] had continued to move
from China to India in payment for opium, but the larger part
of the export from India after the early fifties was purchased
by means of bills on London; in Jardine's case, bills drawn on
their affiliate, Matheson and Company.

In this way the triangular pattern underwent great change
in direction and content. Payment to China was increasingly
dependent upon the out-turn in London of past tea and silk
investments with a more direct trade pattern gradually emerging.
The Indian revenue and the opium trade ceased to be the most
essential factors in China's export trade; even in the fifties
the problem of a suitable return, from Europe, had become
urgent.

Marx, among other contemporary observers, overestimated
the volume of Western goods selling in China, thereby assuming
that handicraft industries were being destroyed and that the
balance of trade was increasingly against China.[20] However, the
archive shows that the drain of precious metals from China
had been stopped and reversed in 1851-1852, and judging by the
firm's account sales it is unlikely that such small quantities
of manufactured goods as were imported, even when multiplied

by the number of foreign firms in China, could have had an influence wide enough to unbalance the traditional economy and cause social distress.[21] Contemporary reports from China mention that a Chinese dressed in foreign cotton was a rare sight, even in the treaty ports.[22] Marx was correct about the trend, but the specific results of Western enterprise in China that eventually confirmed his analysis were those of the twentieth century.

To stay heavily in opium investment, carriage, and sale through the middle decades of the nineteenth century, was there-fore, for a firm of Jardine's character, a decision dictated by the objective circumstances of the China trade. An examination of the firm's organization of this part of its business must precede the study of other activity.

The firm gave close attention to the negotiations in 1842 and 1843 because it wished to secure the opium trade from the possible interference of the British government through the British navy.[23] Partners argued that Britain's supply of tea and Indian government revenues depended upon continued trade in the only commodity for which there was steady demand in China, and that a British decision to police Chinese waters would result in lower tea revenues while opium profits would go to the nationals of other states. These arguments were repeated many times[24] and there was thus great satisfaction when opium was not mentioned in the crucial Supplementary Treaty of October 1843. Sir Henry Pottinger's subsequent proclamation as plenipotentiary, forbidding opium imports at the treaty ports, amounted to an assurance of immunity for receiving ships outside the limits of the ports.[25]

During the negotiations the firm had changed its stand on the question of legalization, then and thereafter the favored

aim of the British government. In the autumn of 1842 Alexander
Matheson's correspondence expressed disapproval of any legalization scheme, yet early in 1843 he seemed to believe that legalization might be useful because it would lower costs and perhaps
dampen the speculative excitement which was attracting many
small dealers from India to Hong Kong.[26] Before the end of
the year, however, and before the Supplementary Treaty was
signed, the firm's position had hardened against legalization.
Matheson wrote that abolition of the smuggling system would
lower delivery costs and thus would certainly increase competition and encourage the "men of small capital" arriving
in China with high hopes for trade under the treaty. Legalization might also have confined opium sales to Hong Kong where
the quasi-monopoly advantages of the coastal system would have
been impossible. A note of relief is evident in the letters
announcing that Ch'i-ying, imperial commissioner in charge
of negotiations, had parried all schemes for legalization
on the grounds that the emperor would not tolerate such a
suggestion.[27]

In the five years before Commissioner Lin's arrival
at Canton the firm had made the bulk of its drug sales along
the Eastern and Southern coasts, away from Whampoa-Canton,
thereby gaining a great advantage over competitors bound to
the Whampoa-Canton or Lintin smuggling centers, where combinations of Chinese brokers and the exactions of experienced
officials lowered profits. There, Chinese brokers who came
out to the receiving ships in "fast boats" normally refused
to bid against each other and often had come to an agreement
before dealing with the foreign merchants. Away from the
Canton estuary the firm could charge prices well above those
allowed by the old market, yet below those quoted by local
Chinese dealers receiving supplies overland or by junk from
Canton.[28]

The war had increased these advantages. During its course, Jardine's share of Indian export was often two-thirds of the total, with prices high. The uncertainty following British exclusion from Canton and the confused nature of reports reaching India, provided excellent opportunities for speculative investments. Success depended upon the firm's coastal fleet which, for a time, operated from Manila, and upon its delivery vessels which ranged from the islands near Hong Kong as far north as Chusan and the Yangtze estuary. The Canton Opium Guild and most European or Parsee competitors either had no supplies or were without the means of delivering them.[29]

The Chinese had first developed the coastal system for smuggling opium.[30] In the 1820's enterprising dealers had purchased drug at Macao, transshipped to coastal junks and sailed north to Swatow or Amoy, thereby avoiding the worst official squeeze and therefore able to sell at higher prices than those prevailing near the source of supply in the South. James Matheson first imitated this plan in the late twenties without much success but it later became normal practice during the decade of rapid growth preceding the war.[31] After the war, the cost of extra shipping, staff, and insurance demanded by coast marketing greatly diminished competition, but did not remove it entirely. Two factors, however, began to favor a large dealer such as Jardine's. First, by investing very heavily some months, and by receiving the bulk of India con-signments, the firm was able to decline all offers at Hong Kong or Lintin and send entire shipments to the coast, thereby commanding the market before rivals could come north to compete. Second, widespread piracy, a further sign of China's administra-tive and economic decay, which seriously menaced opium vessels and called for extra crew or heavy armament, increased overhead,

favored firms with large capital, and discouraged many from
risking shipment in unarmed vessels or in native junks.

So successful was the coastal system for a large firm
that Jardine's considered a shift of all its opium business
to the north in 1844. Correspondence with Matheson and Company
stressed the importance of the hinterland of Shanghai-Woosung,
the Yangtze provinces, where opium sales had doubled in eight
months and proposed the concentration of supplies on three
receiving ships at Woosung where a resident manager had been
appointed to handle the business in cooperation with the opium
captains. By this move, Jardine's recognized the vital importance
of Shanghai's location, and avoided older centers of the trade,
such as Lintin, Namoa, or Amoy, where the Chinese often combined
to delay business and bring down prices.[32] However, the firm
was flexible and would revert to sales in Whampoa or Lintin when
low supplies or brisk demand allowed:

> We hope your constituents will be as well satisfied as
> you anticipate by our appropriating to them a share in our
> coast sales. They will find, however, on occasion, that
> sales in the Canton River or here (Hongkong) will give a
> better net result owing to the necessarily high charges
> for the coast.[33]

These charges followed from the high cost of maintaining (in
1845) fourteen receiving ships along the coast, one at Hong Kong,
and four clipper ships to carry supplies between them. Average
annual costs of the system totaled between $250,000 and $300,000,
none of which, the firm maintained, was passed on to shippers
in India so long as the policy of bulk sales at regular intervals
continued to bring good profits.[34] Jamsetjee Jeejeebhoy and
Company, Bombay, with whom the firm conducted joint-account

business of £1,000,000 annual value in the 1830's,[35] com-
plained in 1846 that Jardine's had not lowered its commission charges on raw cotton or opium in accord with
those of many smaller dealers, particularly the Parsees who
speculated in small amounts at Hong Kong or Canton. The firm
replied that big operations required more capital: "In former
times when he had an establishment at Canton only, these commission charges were not considered high. Now we are compelled
to keep branches at Canton, Macao, Shanghai and Amoy besides
our coast stations, involving a very heavy outlay of capital
and large annual disbursements."[36]

An expensive establishment of branches in the new ports,
paralleling the coast system and meant for legitimate trade, had
rested on hopes of an expanding market for British manufactured
goods and on the expectation that tea and silk exports would
naturally center in good ports near the producing areas as soon
as internal trade had broken out of the artificial channels
created by the Canton System. But the "Canton Interest," those
ex-hong merchants, officials, and provincial middlemen who had
handled the export of tea and silk as well as the opium import
under the old system, continued to divert trade from "natural"
channels until the late forties when many of them had established
themselves as allies of the Western merchants at the new Yangtze-
coastal entrepot, Shanghai.[37] Consequently, legitimate agencies
at each of the new ports were a considerable expense in the late
forties, an expense exacerbated by increasing competition in
opium sales on the coast: "Competition has ruined the opium
trade for a time and we must wait for the trade to ruin our
competitors."[38] By 1845, the expensive coastal system, combined
with support from agents in India, had begun to thin out this
new competition, leaving most of the field to Jardine's and Dent

and Company whose duopoly became the arbiter of opium prices in China.[39]

The two firms had permitted cooperation between their respective captains at the coastal stations since the 1830's, although this was not a continuous policy on either side. If a station found itself oversupplied the temptation to under-sell was not often resisted and there was considerable re-crimination on this score. Normally, however, they acted in combination against other competitors. Their captains would anchor near third parties to lower prices in concert, sustaining losses if necessary until they had driven smaller dealers from the station. Experience was their most valuable asset as both firms were known and trusted by Chinese dealers willing to accept their drug without examination, and they were in a position to forbid most Chinese buyers to deal with other smugglers.[40] As a result, Jardine's and Dent's shared the opium market on the coast until 1850.[41]

Thus the operation of Jardine Matheson's system became almost routine after 1846. Each month instructions were sent from the head office at Hong Kong to "the Commanders of Jardine Matheson and Company vessels, Southern and Eastern Stations," which included all receiving ships on the coast, ranging from fourteen in 1845 to ten in 1851, the average number for the next decade.[42] A fortnightly clipper, one to the south and one to the east, would leave Hong Kong "Cumsingmun," an anchorage near Hong Kong, or Lintin to deliver the drug at each of the receiving stations along the coast. There was no Chinese navy to interfere and the clippers were heavily armed against pirates. On the return voyage the clipper would collect proceeds from each station in the form of sycee or gold coin which would be divided at Hong Kong, part transshipped for India and part retained in China.[43]

Instructions to commanders were normally collective and gave a general picture of the Hong Kong market before issuing orders on sales:

> The almost simultaneous arrival of (four) vessels from the fifth and sixth Calcutta sales has caused, for the moment, a panic among the dealers and prices which had previously been well supported at our last quotations have given way....After a time, however, the market will probably rally somewhat, but, for the present you will continue to take full share of sales at current rates.[44]

The firm's monthly Opium Circular was compiled from each commander's formal monthly reports which provide a review of daily business at the stations.[45] These reports show that a common system prevailed on the coast except at Woosung-Shanghai whose rapid development as an opium station paralleled its growth as the most important center of legitimate trade. By 1850 Woosung-Shanghai had become the focus of the opium business and its accounts dwarf those of other stations. One letter states: "You will please bear in mind that money in China has been scarce for some time back, and as we are dependent upon the Woosung station for a considerable portion of our supplies, it would be most inconvenient were we entirely deprived of these."[46] The expected shift of trade to the north had begun and the firm's average monthly sales on the coast of 600 chests were divided almost evenly between Woosung, which required 350 chests, and all other stations. From Woosung the drug was presumably distributed along the Yangtze and northward by the junk fleets.

The coastal system constituted an illegal market, yet until the mid-fifties commanders' reports show that Woosung and other stations conducted legal trade aboard receiving vessels with the same Chinese dealers who purchased opium. Although

Jardine's had established offices and godowns in Shanghai, this
practice of mixing legal with illegal trade seems to have arisen
as a matter of convenience during the growth of silk exports
from Shanghai. Chinese opium dealers, accepting delivery at
Woosung, would pay in silver to agents of a Shanghai silk dealer.
Sometimes the latter was also a member of the local Opium Guild
and had previously delivered silk to a nearby Jardine vessel.
This saved shoffrage and other miscellaneous charges, but it
indicates that the coastal system was not a lasting solution
to the problem of a trade in which one of the most important
elements, opium, remained contraband while contributing to the
operations of the whole.

In its capacity as agent the firm had in the three
middle decades, 1840-1870, more than 150 correspondents in
Calcutta, Bombay and Madras. Three of these correspondents were
most important because of the size of their business in opium
and their ability to influence smaller firms in India:
Jeejeebhoy and Company, Bombay, Remington and Company, Bombay,
and Jardine, Skinner, Calcutta.[47] Jeejeebhoy and Company, a
Parsee firm at the heart of the commerce of Western India, had
long specialized in China trading through the export of Malwa
opium and raw cotton. Remington and Company, one of the oldest
British firms in Bombay, was associated with Jeejeebhoy in the
cotton business throughout India and did a large business
selling British cotton goods in Bombay.[48] Both firms had joined
with Jardine's in an informal Malwa Opium Syndicate which
functioned for thirty years.[49]

The government-controlled Bengal monopoly provided
regular reports and irregular memoranda on crops and possible
yields in the Benares and Behar agencies, but Jardine's depended

upon Jeejeebhoy and others for its knowledge of the Malwa
crop and Bombay market trends in order to prepare instructions
to commanders on the coast.[50] David Jardine wrote Jeejeebhoy
that this information made the coast system workable by giving
the firm a counterweight to the combinations of the Chinese
dealers. A reliable estimate of possible supplies permitted
transfer of opium ships or stockpiling of the drug in anticipation of predicted changes in supply.[51]

To gather this information, Jeejeebhoy and Remington
sent agents to the Native States of Central India and to
Rajputana, but they did not buy or advance on crops in villages.
The agents left finance to a special group of Bombay firms,
specialists in speculation, sometimes described as landowners
or money-lenders.[52] Jardine's associates acted as brokers
only, one link between the agrarian economy of India and that
of China, part of the long chain running from a Rajputana
poppy field tended by a ryot to an opium shop in a Kwangtung
village. That neither of Jardine's principal Bombay associates
bought directly in the poppy-growing areas, or risked advances
there, is of cardinal importance in understanding the firm's
later loss of a market in China and its decision to withdraw
from the opium trade.

There was no legal bond between Jardine, Skinner and
Company, Calcutta, and Jardine, Matheson and Company, but the
latter conducted more business on joint-account in opium with
Calcutta than with Bombay. The whole of Jardine's own investment in Patna and Benares drug, averaging $100,000 monthly in
some periods, was made through Jardine, Skinner and Company,
and all of the latter's own shipments to Hong Kong were on
joint-account with Jardine's.[53] Jardine, Skinner also informed
the China firm about the monthly auctions, watched market trends,

and forwarded the official reports of the government opium
agencies. Indian government supervision of growth and deliberate
control of supply made judgment of the Calcutta market an easier
task than judgment of Malwa market conditions since there were
frequent government reports to the Office of the Board of Revenue
in Calcutta.[54] Jardine, Skinner also forwarded crop reports
from the divisions of each agency, and these, with government
reports, contributed to the careful working of the coastal
system. Each of the India agents also canvassed for consignments to Jardine's, using their shipping and insurance services
as an inducement to opium exporters in their areas.

The counterpart to the agency reports and the informal
replies of Jeejeebhoy and Remington was the monthly Jardine
Opium Circular sent out from China. It followed a set form
and went to all "friends" on the opium list during these twenty
years. It normally began with general remarks, sometimes
commenting cautiously about political events in China, and then
described current markets for each type of opium (Woosung
received special notice for the benefit of Malwa shippers in
Bombay), quoted average prices, estimated current stocks
in China, and gave current exchange rates for India and London.[55]
Relations with opium firms in India were thus mutually self-
supporting to a high degree, as the trade demanded constant
study and accurate assessment and the support of these India
houses was Jardine, Matheson and Company's indispensable link
with the early stages of supply.[56] However, as I shall point
out Jardine's allowed the informal character of their mutual
support to persist into the period of close organization after
1860 possibly because an early start in the trade had generated
a certain complacency about India where old methods had worked
well for decades. Though the firm could react quickly to any
change in trade conditions on the China coast, it could not

control its India agents and seems not to have understood the
nature of the trade's agrarian base.

        Cantonese merchants became the natural allies of
Western commercial agents in their attempt to expand operations
in China after 1842 because they had had the longest experience
in dealing with Western merchants. They acted as compradores,
interpreters, shroffs, and clerks. (Some, including former
hong merchants, established their own firms to deal with foreign
imports.)[57] Each Jardine receiving ship had an opium compradore
or an interpreter and a shroff.[58] The head office in Hong Kong
had a large Chinese staff for the auxiliary services of the
opium trade: shipping repairs, warehousing, and accounting. In
1844 the firm rewarded two Cantonese clerks for their help in
negotiating a difficult barter arrangement at Woosung[59] and
by the mid-fifties there were compradores at Woosung, one of
whom specialized in opium and supervised payment for and delivery
of large monthly sales. In keeping with Chinese business practice,
out of which compradorism had evolved, he assumed full liability
for transactions arranged by him or his own staff.[60]
        On the Chinese side of the trade daily operations in
the drug continued to depend upon the willingness of Chinese
dealers to face the risk and expense of a nominally illegal
trade. That they were willing to take such risks regularly is
an indication of good profits in Chinese markets. The Jardine,
Matheson papers say little about organization of the trade within
China probably because in the halcyon days of large shipments
and high profits there was no need for attention to the nature
of the Chinese market. Only when the Taiping Rebellion began
to interfere with demand did the firm comment on the Chinese side
of the trade and then they simply concluded that Chinese dealers

could not supply areas where the imperial administration no
longer existed since official approval, or Taiping hostility,
apparently determined conditions of distribution and sale.
This conclusion tells little about Chinese organization of the
trade beyond the fact that many officials, in conditions of
economic stagnation or collapse, had come to depend upon revenue
from opium sales in their area or from opium in transit.[61]
It is probably correct to assume that official participation
was an important factor in demand because it would embolden
Chinese dealers who would not risk investment except in the
context of official support. But this does not allow us to be
specific about internal markets.

The archive, therefore, indicates that, although
concerned about internal trade during that rebellion, foreign
merchants had a remarkably vague store of information about
Chinese commerce away from the treaty ports or the receiving
stations; dealers in these areas as in the treaty ports were
known to engage in foreign trade as members of local guilds,
frequently ready to combine in efforts to obtain price re-
ductions. But Jardine's did not record details about opium
or other business arrangements between the brokers on the
coast and the hinterland. When an unusually heavy demand for
Malwa appeared at Woosung in the summer of 1851, the result
of an unexpectedly large number of grain junks leaving for
Peking via the Grand Canal, each with a share of the drug,
Jardine's learned too late for firmer pricing, and mentioned
that it was impossible to prepare for such windfalls.[62] The
Chinese guilds would not, apparently, enlighten foreign merchants
about the movements of internal trade and there are some signs
that compradores found it more profitable to remain silent
also.[63] Organized guilds of Chinese dealers not only controlled distribution; they also competed in coastal sales,

as at Swatow where the local Opium Guild frequently bought
supplies at Hong Kong from Parsee importers (Chinese were
thought to be heavy investors at Calcutta auctions and
Bombay sales through these same agents)[64] and delivered
them by junk or Peninsular and Oriental steamer on the coast.
The guild also reportedly first mixed China-grown drugs with
Indian imports, a practice believed to have stimulated home
production and foreign imports as it became widespread in
the fifties.[65]

   In this way, through twenty years, the work of the
Chinese staff with foreign firms and the activity of Chinese
merchant guilds and some officials had contributed to the
expansion of the opium trade, though the nature of the trade,
nominally illegal and very profitable, the political and
economic chaos within China, and the competition between
guilds and Western firms prevented the development of more
extensive cooperation and interdependence in trade, such as
began to characterize Western enterprise in China after 1865.

   Chinese merchants and agents engaged with Jardine's
in the opium trade represented one nucleus of the modern
Chinese business class. When the Taiping Rebellion collapsed
and the country began to recover economically, these men
moved into many positions in foreign trade formerly commanded
by foreigners. They engaged in the import of cotton piece
goods and the organization of the export trade; in the
treaty ports they were investors in native banks and pawnshops.[66] A large amount of capital was assumed to be in
their hands but there was little inducement or opportunity
to use this capital in other than traditional ways before
1870 because large Western firms, intent on opium and
exports, had organized relatively few investment opportunities

in the modern sector, the treaty ports. Those that existed
had been well supported by Chinese investors, an indication
that a good deal more could have been done.[67] Only when
profits of the Indian opium trade began to decline[68] and
China firms of Jardine's size and stature virtually withdrew
from it, did there appear a series of new business ideas.
Coinciding with the restriction of investment opportunities
throughout the world, withdrawal from the opium trade left
the firm free to initiate new projects and encouraged a new
spirit of cooperation with Chinese capital. But the full
development of these changes came only when Jardine's and
a few other large Western firms, had ceased to be primarily
dealers in commodities on their own account.

Between 1860 and 1872 Jardine's handled each year
greater amounts of opium than ever before. It invested large
sums of its own capital and extended sales, legitimately,
into the heart of China and north of Shanghai; and yet, by
1873, the firm was no longer an important opium dealer in
either China or India.[69] This move out of the trade illustrates the effects of an improved communications system and
offers a partial explanation of the firm's increased emphasis
upon contributory services, its willingness to invest in
such enterprises as railways, and the wide diversification
of its interests in China after the 1870's.

Opium legalization proposals, put forward in the
Tientsin negotiations, had been accepted calmly by the
firm's partners who realized that Chinese-produced opium
had begun to undersell Indian; open sales at established
agencies seemed the only way to compete with increased
supplies of Chinese drug.[70] But the most pertinent result

of legalization was the importance given to the organization
of the trade in India. After 1860, all dealers in China,
regardless of experience, faced the same tax and the growing
competition of Chinese drug, so that prices and costs in
India became crucial to continued success in the trade.[71]

As anticipated, legalization stimulated demand in
China for both Indian and Chinese varieties of drug and
from 1860 to 1864 the former commanded steady or rising
prices though the Chinese drug was becoming less coarse and
more widely circulated. The market for both kinds seemed
limitless.[72] In 1861 Malwa was selling at the highest price
in twenty years (Tls. 840 per picul),* while Jardine's sales
at Amoy alone, a relatively minor opium market, totalled
Tls. 190,000.00.[73] In this buoyant market the firm had
invested heavily on its own account, while handling close
to £300,000 worth of drug annually on commission each year
through 1865.[74] Until that year correspondence reflected
reasonable confidence in India agents and constituents,
although there was some complaint about prices and volumes,
especially about cost control which became urgent because of
the coordinated buying of a group centered around David
Sassoon and Sons of Bombay and Hong Kong.

Sassoon's had specialized in the export of raw cotton
to Britain and China for many years and, from the founding
of the firm in the late eighteenth century,[75] had also been
in opium through loans to producers in the Native States of
India, loans which were recovered with interest at the sales

---

*In 1864, 1 Tl. equaled 6 shillings, 8 pence, or about
$1.60. One picul is equal to 133 1/3 lbs.

of Malwa in Bombay.[76] Jardine's manifests show that
Sassoon's was also shipping opium to China on its own
account from 1834 or perhaps earlier[77] and shortly after
Hong Kong had become a colony, David Sassoon opened a
branch which concentrated upon opium business. Since his
firm was already established in Calcutta and Singapore, he
had a branch at that time at every link in the India-China
opium chain except in the coastal system.[78] This link was
provided by the extension of Peninsular and Oriental Steamship Company's services on the coast in the early fifties.

The first signs of strong new competition occurred in
the mid-fifties when Sassoon sales on the coast were linked
with increasing speculation at the Bombay sales.[79] G.M.
Robertson of Jardine, Skinner, reported that Sassoon
associates (E. Gubbay and Company, E.D.I. Ezra and Company,
S. Isaac, all of Calcutta) were also buying in agreement
at the Calcutta auctions, and, during the stages of the
second war, this group had been strong enough to support
prices of Bengal drug by buying at high levels and holding
their stock for some time in China.[80] By 1860, Jardine's
was fully aware of the importance of prices in India and
had recognized the threat this group represented. From that
year the Sassoon group began to make use of methods adopted
by Jardine's and Dent's in the thirties and forties, bulk
sales at low rates combined with advances to Chinese dealers
and regular deliveries. The expanding market enabled them
to use their methods with great effect.

However, the real strength of the Sassoon group lay in
their practice of advancing as high as three-quarters of
costs to Indian dealers willing to consign shipments on a
regular basis. Jardine's associates in India attempted the

same but, as their advances were provided through large agency houses in Bombay and Calcutta, they failed to affect the producing areas where Sassoon's purchased unharvested poppy crops through experienced agents.[81] Jardine's associates retained a number of advantages, however, since they advanced, at a favorable rate of rupees for dollars in the Bombay market and the Calcutta auctions, the dollars payable in China from the proceeds of the sale. Also, drug could be shipped in one of the firm's vessels, at a reduced rate, and insured by one of the firm's managed companies such as the Bengal Insurance Society. This substantial pool of services and the great reputation of the firm continued to attract shippers through the late sixties, but Jardine's could not finally compete successfully with the Sassoon system of crop purchases in the Malwa-producing districts of India.

Sassoon's methods were so successful that by 1871 Jardine's had only one considerable account, Rustomjee Eduljee and Company, Bombay, and had ceased to invest its own capital regularly in opium.[84] Several letters advised Eduljee to purchase in the producing districts, rather than Bombay, and encouraged him in an abortive attempt to organize an opium syndicate, similar to Sassoon's, among Parsee firms.[85] He was not successful and in that year there were many changes of plan; one letter announced Jardine's withdrawal from the trade except in the provision of services connected with it, and the next advised agents in Calcutta and Bombay that the firm would advance loans to secure consignments "as the market for drug continues to expand." Early in 1871, the Sassoon group was acknowledged to be the major holder of opium stocks in India and in China; they were owners

and controllers of 70 per cent of the total of all kinds.[86]
Their superiority had probably been established in the
previous year because a major part of Malwa listed as the
property of various Malwarese merchants in 1870 was actually
owned by members of the Sassoon group from the time of
planting.[87] Strict control of costs in India had allowed
the group to undersell all others in China for five years
and against this organization Jardine's was defenseless;
its withdrawal from the trade became inevitable as its
partners realized that to stay would require a renewed
concentration of resources and managerial skills which the
firm could muster only by neglecting other interests, now
of paramount importance. A letter to Remington and Company
remarked that the firm "now looked to opium only for
freight, charges, insurance and storage."[88] The collapse
of the Eduljee firm in November 1872, marked the end of
Jardine, Matheson and Company's large dealings in opium.

Opium had provided the capital reserve essential to
survival and growth in a precarious economic environment,
lubricated the export trade, stimulated the improvement of
communications, and probably provided China firms with a
surplus to invest in world markets. Decades of concentration
upon the trade had conditioned the whole nature of Western
enterprise in China.

Profit from opium had averaged an estimated 15 per cent
on the firm's own investments and 4 per cent on agency
business during the fifties and sixties.[89] With these
profits Jardine's had built the structure needed to sustain
the trade and to finance its investment in tea and silk.
Silver sycee and gold taken in payment for opium had
provided commissions on exchange services and loan business

in the treaty ports was usually financed from opium profit.
The great Property Account, growing each season, reflected
the investment of these profits in shore establishments,
docks, and warehouses.[90]

Although the whole of the firm's early investment in
the service of trade had turned upon the pivot of opium
and commercial growth within the treaty ports was undoubtedly stimulated by this constant investment in structure,
trade in drug also had the effect of channeling a major
part of the commercial enterprise of several large Western
and Indian firms in China into the sale and servicing
of one commodity for several decades. There was no
practical alternative before the 1870's. It was not until
the firm had been forced from the trade as a major partici-
pant that it began proposing the use of capital and techniques for many alternative investments in the treaty ports
and in the domestic Chinese economy. Opium had been the
indispensable commodity. When it became a trade of declining
importance and diminishing profits, the firm withdrew
easily, focusing its enterprise upon new opportunities in
the changing China trade of the 1870's.

Chapter II

THE COTTON TRADE

The history of the India-China raw cotton trade is of
interest because it illustrates the nature of China's pre-
modern economy. From the late eighteenth century until 1823
raw cotton was the major Indian export to China, where it was
used in village hand-loom industries as a small supplement to
China's own vast crops. After opium replaced raw cotton as
China's major import in 1823, the volume of cotton imported
(442,640 piculs in 1833 and 335,976 piculs in 1867) showed
little change through the rest of the century.[1] The Chinese
were able to supply their own needs. In the years immediately
after 1842, opium and raw cotton were still referred to as
"the two great staples of the import trade" and Jardine's,
true to its character as an agency house, accepted cotton on
consignment from its chief correspondents in Bombay, Calcutta,
and Madras. Jeejeebhoy and Company was the most important
shipper of both commodities in the fifties; cotton, like opium,
was consigned to Jardine-managed ships and sold in the treaty
ports on the basis of a 3 per cent commission if Chinese demand
responded to supplies, bartered against tea if it did not.[2]
    The significant difference between cotton and opium was the
firm's lack of confidence in sustained Chinese demand for the
former, so that very large shipments began to be accepted only
when their principal opium associates, heavily involved in
cotton-production and trade in India, pressed for the acceptance
of both commodities. Jeejeebhoy, particularly, harked back to
short-term cotton booms of earlier days and expected increasing

sales in a newly opened China although by the late forties his
cotton was being used mainly for barter against tea and silk.[3]
"A nominal price was agreed upon between buyer and seller for
the convenience of account keeping but this almost always had
reference to the return investment in tea or other produce."[4]
Jardine's accepted tea, silk, and sugar in order to move
Jeejeebhoy's shipments[5] and only when their compradores or
Chinese merchants reported severe damage to Chinese crops,
particularly the "Nanking crop" of the Yangtze valley, was the
firm willing to act in raw cotton on its own account. These
investments never exceeded $250,000 per annum and were usually
much less.[6]

India houses, however, continued to consign, though
the archive shows that extreme fluctuation in demand and falling
volume were major characteristics of the trade in the fifties,
especially after the Taiping rebels had marched; Chinese dealers
would stop business at each report of "an insurgent advance."
The firm made most of its sales for Jeejeebhoy at Amoy from which
the village cloth industries of Fukien were supplied during the
rebellion. Within Fukien carriage costs for imported staple
seem to have been reasonable,[7] but even at Amoy demand was weak,
the market requiring two months to absorb three thousand bales.[8]

By 1853 Shanghai had become the best general market
in spite of the administrative chaos of the city. The majority
of the cotton sold there found its ultimate sale several hundred
miles up the Yangtze, in Hupeh and Honan, where, according to
Chinese dealers, its price compared favorably with Chinese
staples.[9] Eventually, Canton, Amoy, and Shanghai took almost
every bale imported. Canton's continued place in the trade
indicates that Indian raw cotton must have come into general
use in some districts of Kwangsi and Kwangtung when the import

of pre-treaty days, following ancient internal trade routes, had built up a small demand.

When Jardine's explained the weakness of Chinese demand for cotton to Indian exporters they often suggested that their Indian associates combine with other large exporters to China in order to regulate production and ensure that shipments be timed to meet stronger markets in China: "If shipments are moderate we can do good here." However, such a scheme seems to have been impractical since in the mid-fifties some twenty thousand bales per month were still being exported from Bombay and roughly half that amount went from Calcutta, far too much for the poor China market.[10]

A Chinese-speaking staff was indispensable for careful negotiations with wary dealers since cotton was often a barter business. Its reports gave the firm an intimation of China's self-sufficiency and the ability of dealers to resist imports which failed to suit Chinese needs. Demand for cotton yarn (apparently adapted to Chinese hand-looms about 1843) also indicated the self-sufficiency and selectivity of the Chinese market.

A further interesting aspect of this trade could be seen during the American Civil War when a group of Chinese merchants in Shanghai, among whom was Jardine's compradore, "Acum," purchased cotton in the Yellow River Valley, away from rebel areas, and offered it for sale in Shanghai.[11] In 1863 and 1864 Jardine's exported almost two million dollars worth of the Chinese crop to the Liverpool market; most of this was very short staple and, according to Matheson and Company, unsuitable and dirty; losses amounted to $280,000 and the firm blamed the negligence of Chinese dealers and their agents who had contracted for this quality in order to profit from stong demand.[12] This venture and two others in 1864-1865, when the firm also acted as agent for Chinese exporters, had the effect of bringing Jardine's into close contact with a group of Shanghai merchants willing to speculate in foreign trade. Some of these merchants joined in later investment activities and are listed as customers of the Jardine "Native Bank" established at Shanghai in 1863.[13]

After the collapse of prices at the end of the American war there was a lag in Jardine's activity in raw cotton until 1868 when recovery from the Taiping Rebellion brought new demand for Indian cotton at Shanghai, Amoy, and Canton. Consignments were accepted again and Indian correspondents were warned, as they had been in the past, that this demand was precarious rather than normal.[14] As expected, persistently low purchasing power plagued the raw cotton trade through the early seventies and later years of general prosperity brought no improvement. Jardine's found the cotton trade like the opium trade passing into the hands of a few India-based firms willing to specialize. "Parsees seem always to undersell us. To help our steamers we have been receiving a monthly invoice of the Staple, but the inevitable result has been to sacrifice part of the freight. We are tired of Indian business."[15] By 1875 after three years of poor sales, the firm's activity in raw cotton had become minimal in keeping with the general decline of interest in India, though it continued to be described ritually for many years as a great staple of the India-China trade.[16]

Fluctuations in this trade raise possibly unanswerable questions about the internal economy. Though there was never a significantly large amount imported, changing demand indicates the general condition of the economy in the coastal regions of the South, which like that of nineteenth-century rural China as a whole, seems to have been "circular-flow," relatively stagnant and self-sustaining, with some years of poor cotton crop totals and increased demand for a temporary supplement.

Like most Western merchants active after the Treaty of Nanking, Jardine's directors had expected Chinese hand-looms and homespun to give way before British machine-made goods, as home industries had done in Europe and India. The collapse of demand in 1845 revealed the stubborn resistance of China's consumers, or their poverty; no one was certain, though explanations abounded.[17]

The only important foreign competition in piece goods before 1860 was Russian. Coarse, strong Russian cloth appeared in the Shanghai market in the early fifties as part of extensive bartering for teas at Shanghai and Hankow and sold at prices well below those usually prevailing for British piece goods,[18] but the major competitors in these goods remained China's own domestic hand producers of cloth who knew the Chinese climate and wove fabrics suitable for it. The firm was aware of these conditions and in the late forties had advised Lancashire correspondents about kinds of cloth most in demand at Shanghai and in its circulars had stressed the need for greater selectivity and greater emphasis upon heavier goods.[19] In Britain, however, the China market continued to be regarded as an extension of India so that quality did not improve, sales stayed uncertain, and volume small.

On the other hand, the complaint, frequently made in nineteenth-century England, that British merchants in China did not favor British exports has no cogency in Jardine's case. In 1843, before buildings were ready, Jardine's had placed a special receiving vessel at Woosung to handle cotton and woolen goods. Their Shanghai manager was in charge[20] and until mid-1845, he reported excellent sales, then a falling market and, in 1846, a stagnant one.[21] He concluded that British goods, priced at two-thirds the cost of local cloth, would not sell because Chinese preferred their own "stouter" cloth[22] and that Chinese dealers would buy only the best quality foreign cloth in such a restricted market. The repute of each "chop," or brand mark, became a serious concern with foreign merchants. Jardine's reported that dealers were dissatisfied with the quality of many consignments and they asked Matheson and Company to warn manufacturers and exporters that the Chinese would not tolerate "second quality" and would discriminate among chops. Poor goods also caused difficulty because Chinese dealers refused to accept them in barter against tea or silk.[23]

Under these conditions, piece goods imports remained at a low volume from 1846 until the Treaty of Tientsin. An official report showed that in 1851 British manufactured goods of a gross value of £1,500,000 had been imported into China as against opium imports valued at £6,000,000, and other India goods (mainly raw cotton) at £1,500,000; it concluded that British goods would not sell widely in China because its own cloth production satisfied the market:[24]

> The Chinese peasant worked his own loom. The Fukien farmer traded his sugar for northern cotton which he then carded, spun and wove into a heavy durable material; after harvest time the entire peasant family was engaged in producing home-spun. Only the hong clerks, the bookeepers and the shopkeepers wore the neater but less durable and more expensive British long cloth.[25]

Jardine's agreed that British cloth was less durable but argued that there would be a market for such goods if they

were not unfairly taxed along interior routes. Yet the firm
had come to substantially the same conclusion in their private
correspondence two years previous to the report, stating that
economic reasons were at least as influential as political in
restricting Chinese demand and inferring that Chinese cloth
would not be easily superseded except near the treaty ports.[26]
The firm stayed in the trade through the fifties and took shipments on joint-account, largely because of the exigencies of
export and shipping. Orders in Manchester were explicitly linked
to the advantage of having goods for barter and, by influencing
consignments from manufacturers and exporters, they were also
linked to the provision of cargo for returning tea vessels
from Liverpool. There were also a few instances noted in the
accounts when Chinese merchants of Shanghai placed orders in
England for piece goods though Jardine's. These were exceptional
in the fifties and appear to have been connected with shipments
to northern provinces.[27] Yet this is a small indication that
Chinese merchants could act as advance agents for Western commerce
by inaugurating the transport and sale of foreign goods in
markets which the latter would attempt to develop at a later date.

The failure of British cotton goods in the China market
until the final quarter of the century was doubly disappointing
since Western demand for tea and silk grew so rapidly in the
late forties and early fifties that even growing opium imports
could not balance the trade and silver again flowed to China.[28]
Jardine's and others could not achieve large volumes because
the goods themselves did not meet Chinese needs or popular price
levels. The firm was then caricatured as a greedy opium monopoly,
disinterested in all other aspects of foreign trade, reluctant
to "push calicoes" because of this failure. However, although
it had never been a pure agency house even in its earliest days

when there had always been enough trading on its own account
to justify describing it as a merchant house and as a commission
agency, its function as an active agent did not cease even in
the interwar years, when large amounts of the partners' capital
and capital deposits had been invested in opium and tea. The
firm was always both a merchant house operating with its own
capital and an agency house whose accounts were still solicited
through Matheson and Company. Partners in China often expressed
their disappointment about China's limited market for British
goods and they confidently predicted a great demand for British
textiles as soon as the rebellion ended.[29] In fact, development in cotton piece goods imports did reflect the changed
pattern of trade between 1860 and the mid-seventies. When agri-
culture recovered in areas which had been devastated by the
rebellion, export crops were restored, Hankow emerged as a
tea center and port, and Chinese demand for piece goods grew.
Demand remained limited to the needs of a very small part
of China's consumers, perhaps only the treaty port commercial
classes, yet, judging by the steady growth of the market during
the last quarter of the century, their tastes seem to have begun
to create an important outlet for Western goods.

Jardine's sales from 1865 followed this rising demand,
focused especially in the new northern and Yangtze treaty
port markets, where orders were solicited more actively than in
previous years.[30] Large consignments were also stored at Hong
Kong and Shanghai (where one-third of each shipment was sold)
ready to meet local demand or be sent to the outports.[31]
However, the larger part of the selling was always done at
Shanghai to a close combination of Chinese dealers whose guild
naturally wanted a concentration of business, an arrangement
accepted by foreign importers when it became evident that

they could not undersell the Chinese dealers who acted as agents of the guild in the outports.[32]

The firm handled just over one million dollars worth of piece goods per annum in the late sixties, and some three million dollars worth per annum in the early seventies.[33] Auction sales with Maitland and Company began at Shanghai in 1872.[34] James Whittall wrote: "There is an upward tendency in piece goods, considerable animation, Chinese dealers confident, and heavy supplies coming forward."[35]

Then, in the middle and late seventies, when the "Great Depression" prevailed, Jardine, Matheson and Company reported again a very weak piece goods market. During these years of poor returns in direct trade between China and Britain, when the previous relative decline of India-China business had set the stage for a change in the main direction of Western enterprise among the larger firms in China, interest began to shift from investment in or commission on the exchange of commodities, raw and manufactured, to a new emphasis on the commercial auxiliaries of trade. The growing strength of the Chinese in the foreign trade of their country during the seventies was both a result of and a catalyst of this process.

Of course this shift did not mean permanent exclusion from the import trade and the firm once more handled large commissioned orders when slow, uncertain, albeit improved, demand for foreign piece goods sometimes enlivened the import side of the trade, especially after 1880. Volume grew slightly each year and the great increase which was concentrated in the years after the war with France was attributable to yarn as well as piece goods, indicating the continued resistance of China's hand-loom industry as well as falling prices for India's machine-made yarn. The firm sold most of its consigned piece goods

at the Shanghai public auctions after 1880, charging 2 per
cent commission, 1/2 per cent more than other houses because
of guaranteed sale and remittance. Out of its commission
Jardine's paid a Chinese broker, boat and coolie hire, landing,
insurance, and shoffrage fees. Correspondence shows that the
firm was cautiously optimistic about piece goods, though frequently mentioning that the depreciation in the value of silver
had added one further burden to "an already difficult trade,"
and indicating that the firm invested only a small amount of
its own capital in piece goods.[36]

It is clear that Chinese buyers did not resist foreign
goods on principle or because there was no need for such
goods; demand was often strong, though purchasing power was
not, even for goods which lacked durability. However, later
yarn sales (equaling piece goods value by 1900) reflected
Chinese determination to make their own cloth in traditional
ways unless kinds and prices of imported goods were suitable.
The difficulties of this trade reflect the poverty of nineteenth-
century China.

In the latter half of the seventies Jardine, Matheson
and Company was also interested in the establishment of cotton
mills in China although there was no explicit provision in the
treaties for foreign-owned factories, even within the concessions, and it was generally assumed that the British government
would not defend the rights of those attempting to test Chinese
intentions.[37] The firm's initial plan, drawn up in 1877, did
not call for Western ownership; rather it followed the
kuan-tu shang-pan ("government supervision, merchant operation")
principle in encouraging the formation of a cotton mill company
under official supervision and Chinese merchant management with

Jardine's using its close industrial and commercial associations
in Britain as agent on behalf of such a Chinese company.

F.B. Johnson suggested to a group of Chinese merchants
that they organize a joint-stock company for the purpose of
building a mill in Shanghai. The suggestion was discussed for
several months into 1878 and Hu Kuang-yung, with whom the firm
had done considerable business, sounded out his friends about
the company, to be called the Anglo-Chinese Shanghai Steam
Cotton Mill Company. The mill was to have 800 looms and initial
capital required would be Tls. 350,000. James Keswick was
reasonably confident of its success: "All I can say at the
moment is that if the scheme be carried through at all we shall
have the business for I do not anticipate that the Chinese will
go to any other firm."[38] But the resistance of Chinese officials
to schemes initiated by foreigners was still much greater than
the firm realized. Merchant friends had been "discussing and
petitioning" through the spring and summer of 1878 until the
appearance, in October, of a petition to Li Hung-chang from
Peng, expectant taotai of Shanghai, which proposed a Chinese-
managed mill.[39]

Peng's petition repeated the still current self-
strengthening thesis, emphasizing, however, the power of wealth
more than military might. He pointed out that foreign cloth had
become one of the principal imports into China, requiring that
millions of taels be sent abroad yearly. To stop this drain,
to enrich Chinese instead of foreigners, Peng recommended the
founding of a Chinese Steam Cotton Mill Company: "By this scheme
I reckon that we shall acquire both profit and influence, and
if the management be adequate, not only will our merchants make
money, but the government also will be enriched. Tls. 500,000
will be raised in shares in the same manner as the capital of the

China Merchants Steam Navigation Company was raised."[40]

Li Hung-chang replied on October 21, 1878, agreeing with Peng's general thesis, mentioning that the emperor had ordered him and Shen Pao-chen (governor-general of Kiangsu, Kiangsi, Anhwei, and superintendent of trade for the southern ports), "to look into the scheme and to obtain reports on it from the Taotai at the Treaty Ports...."[41] The reports showed that a mill "would not only have no ill effect on the resources of the poor [ruin domestic handicraft] but would get hold of the profits at present made by foreigners."[42] He approved the details of Peng's scheme: a cotton factory at Shanghai with the newest machinery, 480 power looms, and foreign instructors. Its cotton goods were to be cheaper than foreign imports and if the company were carefully managed it would increase the wealth of China. Peng further petitioned to say that foreign workmen could easily be obtained from Europe and capital raised among the merchant community, although "the difficulty lay in inspiring the multitude with confidence."[43] Li again replied, approving Peng as manager and Peng's suggestions for assistant managers. Cheng Kuan-ying was named joint manager "as he is a man in whom both foreign and Chinese merchants have long reposed confidence."[44] Jardine, Matheson and Company offered at once to help the new Chinese company obtain machinery and personnel. They were told that their offer was under consideration.

In preparing for possible agency, Jardine's carefully considered the technical problems and supplied information to Peng and his group.[45] At their request the firm ascertained the probable market for cotton yarn, Numbers 16 and 20, at Hong Kong and Amoy, and Platt Brothers and Company of Oldham were notified that machines and personnel would soon be needed;

We write regarding the subject of supplying the Chinese
with the plant of Machinery requisite for the establishment
here of a Manufactory by which Native Cotton can be worked
up into Grey Shirtings. This undertaking has so far advanced
that certain influential Chinese have now come forward and
are seeking the necessary permission from the Native
Officials to form themselves into a Company for the purpose
of carrying out the Scheme...we may be called upon at an
early date to definitely state the terms upon which we will
undertake to supply the plant of Machinery....Telegraph to
us the total cost in Sterling including Freight & Insurance
to Shanghai....(The plant must be capable of turning out
270,000 pieces of Grey Shirtings per annum.) On receipt
of your telegram we shall be in a better position to treat
decidedly with the promoters...send by mail a memo of the
probable Wages you would have to arrange for when engaging
the following Skilled hands, viz 1 Chief Superintendent,
1 Engineer, 1 Supt. for carding and spinning machinery,
1 Supt. for the weaving machinery, 1 Mechanic to erect
and set up the Plant & Machinery ready for us. All for three
years....This letter we forward open through our London
friends Messers. Matheson & Co.[46]

In the spring of 1879, however, Peng informed Jardine's
that because of delays their help would not be required for some
time.[47] It became increasingly evident that the prospectus of
"The Shanghai Cotton Spinning & Weaving Company" had failed to
attract sufficient support among treaty port Chinese despite its
appeal to "patriotic" merchants, a promised dividend of 28 1/2
per cent, command of the entire Chinese market, and an un-
specified government subsidy to ensure success.[48] F.B. Johnson
continued to hope that "we shall succeed in working into cotton

manufacture on account of the Chinese Authorities"[49] and through 1880-1881 the firm offered agency services for a government-sponsored mill. Johnson realized why any mill project would be delayed, writing: "It is evident that the Mill, if started, will mainly have to compete with Native manufacturing industry and this is just what Li and Shen, its patrons, do not want to do."[50]

Finally, exasperated by the evident failure of the government scheme, a group of foreign merchants in Shanghai, with Jardine's participating, organized another joint-stock cotton mill company in November, 1882.[51] Their prospectus provoked a protest from the taotai of Shanghai and resulted in an exchange of letters between the Shanghai consular body and Tso Tsung-tang, the new governor-general of Kiangsu, Kiangsi, and Anhwei, on the question of the Western right to establish manufacturing plants in China. The taotai maintained that foreigners had no right to engage in cotton manufacturing in opposition to the officially sponsored Chinese company. Tso supported the taotai in his reply to British protests, arguing that if the manufacture of cotton goods was permitted, then silk, satin, and the reeling-off of cocoons might follow and destroy the livelihood of many Chinese in the city and countryside. He requested the consuls to instruct their nationals to abstain from such works and the Tsungli Yamen repeated his request.

The consular body replied that they declined to admit the right of the Chinese government to prohibit such industries, and that the matter must be settled by discussion between Western diplomats and the Tsungli Yamen in Peking, not by the fiat of local authorities.[52] William Paterson wrote that "there does not seem to be any danger of their absurd pretensions

being given effect to."[53] However, subsequent correspondence
showed that the firm was far from certain of their legal
right to build factories in China and even less certain of
the support of British officials on this point. Apparently
the Shanghai consular staff was not representative of all
diplomatic opinion. Later, Paterson wrote:

> Do not calculate too assuredly upon the protection
> to be given us by the Diplomatic Body at Peking. The
> rights of foreigners in respect to such enterprises
> are not in any way clearly set forth in the Treaties.
> I mean if the Chinese insist upon placing their own
> construction upon the wording of Treaties and appeal
> to their rights under the usual principles of Inter-
> national Law I do not feel sure that the contention of
> foreigners to enjoy special privileges in the settlements
> which are denied to natives, unless expressly granted
> in the Treaties, would be sustained by our own Government,
> considering the present drift of its policy.[54]

Yet growing sales of Bombay yarn indicated that good
profit would be had from establishing factories in the Shanghai
settlement. Therefore, F.B. Johnson recommended that proposed
manufacturing enterprise in the treaty ports should not be
defended by appeals to the treaties or by demands for a clarifica-
tion of legal rights since this would play into the hands of
"anti-progressive" officials and of the foreign diplomats who
resented any further extension of foreign mercantile rights in,
or outside, the treaty ports.[55] Missionary work in the interior
was providing more than enough resentment; foreign diplomats
were afraid they would arouse more antiforeign feeling in both
the people and officials by encouraging factories. Johnson
felt that the wisest course would be to continue organizing

joint-stock enterprises with Chinese investors for those needs--
cotton manufacture and silk reeling--which appeared likely to
render good profits because of changes in domestic and foreign
demand.[56] To do this it was essential to secure the participation
of Chinese merchants, particularly those who, like Hu Kuang-yung
were wealthy and well connected among the bureaucracy yet preferred
not to risk capital in another kuan-tu shang-pan enterprise.
Of the projects themselves, he wrote: "I would recommend that
the interests be tacitly allowed to grow until they become
too extensive to be interfered with without inviting claims for
compensation if disturbed."[57]

This subtle approach to the problem of bureaucratic
obstructiveness ignored the determination of Chinese officials
to prevent merchant participation in foreign-controlled schemes,
which many sincerely believed would injure the livelihood of
the common people and further weaken China. Others, undoubtedly,
realized that industrial projects managed by foreign merchants
would be beyond the reach of the "squeeze" system so vital to
many official incomes.

However, official resistance did not dampen the firm's
interest in cotton mill schemes. Typical of these schemes was
an abortive 1889 plan to organize a cotton-spinning mill at
Shanghai in cooperation with a Bombay yarn merchant: "if he
can get up sufficient capital I shall endeavor to get a company
formed entirely Chinese, with a separate agreement appointing
Jardine, Matheson and Company as Managers for a small percentage
on gross, say 2%,"[58] an arrangement which would honor China's
prohibition of foreign-owned factories while fitting into the
firm's agency structure. Later, when Li Hung-chang's kuan-tu
shang-pan company erected a mill at Shanghai, Jardine's offered
to accept its management in case outside help was needed; this
offer was also declined.

Five years later, in June, 1894, in order to test China's prohibition of foreign-owned manufacturing plants at a time when tension between China and Japan seemed likely to bring war, the firm began to order cotton-spinning machinery from Platt Brothers of Oldham. The first shipment was regarded as a test case and liable to confiscation but "if it succeeds we will order more machinery at once to build a Mill on our property behind the Ningpo Wharf, Shanghai." Another joint-stock company would be organized since "We could get the whole of the capital from the Chinese Piece Goods dealers in Shanghai" and the proposal would make it clear that no official would be included in the company's directorship because "the dealers would not put a tael in any mill where the official element appears." Twenty years of kuan-tu shang-pan enterprise had convinced the firm that Chinese capitalists would no longer tolerate any compromise with official power: "The time has come to exercise our rights."[59]

If the shipment failed there were two ways outlined for disposal of the machinery, to sell it to the Chinese mill or to return it to makers at a reduction and, through the British government, to put in a claim on the Chinese government for any loss. The correspondence does not indicate the outcome of this test, soon dwarfed by war, but the Jardine-managed "Ewo Cotton Spinning and Weaving Company" opened in May, 1897, after the Japanese had secured manufacturing "rights" for all foreigners in the treaty of Shimonoseki.[60] Demoralized and defeated, the bureaucracy had to yield privileges which they had withheld from Western entrepreneurs since the first Opium War.

Chapter III

YEARS OF TRANSITION IN TRADE

The sixties brought great changes in the conduct of
the China trade. The gradual restoration of order after the
lengthy second Opium War and the defeat of the rebellions,
the opening of the Yangtze to foreign shipping and the interior
to foreign merchants, the continuous rise in volume of exports
apparently without fundamental change in the traditional
methods of production and marketing, and the impact of improved
communications with European and American markets changed the
direction of Western enterprise.

During these years large Western firms began to evolve
into managing agencies concerned more with the "external
economies" of trade--shipping, insurance, treaty port utilities,
and banking--than with the buying and selling of commodities.
Jardine, Matheson and Company's withdrawal from the opium
trade, though only indirectly caused by events in China,
and its reluctance to invest on its own account in commodities,
indicate the new direction of Western enterprise in the late
sixties and early seventies. The change was summarized by a
senior partner of Russell and Company in 1872: "When the
period of transition is over, no doubt most of the larger firms
with capital and credit will have transferred themselves from
produce to industrial and financial enterprise and will
become, in fact, private bankers."[1] In the same year, a Jardine
partner wrote: "I believe legitimate development is towards
a permanent revenue by commission accounts and the avoidance
of large produce operations on our sole interest."[2]

Though Jardine's had been interested in shipping, insurance, and exchange since its earliest days, mainly as an adjunct of the drug trade, only in the sixties did these services acquire autonomous importance to the firm, an importance firmly established by the mid-seventies. The firm then began to act on the assumption that increasingly poor returns on direct investment in trade would continue, that Chinese mercantile competition would increase rather than diminish, and that investment in and management of ancillary services was the soundest policy.

Such an evolution into a pure commission agency in commodities, favoring investment in and management of auxiliary services, can be seen in retrospect as a shrewd "self-preserving" response to the recovery of China's economy from the damage of civil war and the revolution in communications between Europe and China, both changes reflected in the increasing influence of Chinese merchants in business areas, heretofore the preserve of Western traders. This was an economic shift few had anticipated after the Treaty of Tientsin when great hopes had been entertained among foreigners about the expected commercial benefits of the opening of the Yangtze and northern ports in 1861. The firm had established branches or agencies at four of nine new ports in 1860-1861, two of which were regular stops for their northern steamers[3] and had joined in the business of the new ports with hope and enthusiasm.[4]

Yet from 1861 to 1864 business at these ports had been only moderately good, because the continued strain of the rebellion upon Chinese commerce made steady trading difficult and profits unsatisfactory. Jardine's felt, however, that the development of new markets was "as good as could be expected while the country is in such an unsettled state."[5] Then, within a year of the Taiping collapse, activity among Chinese

merchants and brokers in the treaty ports indicated that the
internal economy, particularly in the region of the Upper
Yangtze, was recovering at a rapid pace. The "Shantung junk
fleet" loading at Shanghai for northern ports was much larger
and in the late sixties consular and Imperial Maritime Customs'
reports spoke of the steady gains in Chinese merchant influence
as the Chinese commercial sector began to recover and grow.

The customs report from Newchwang in 1865 described
what had begun to happen in the outports of Shanghai, a process
similar to that occurring in the formerly dependent ports of
Hong Kong in the South. Most foreign agencies established in
1860 had withdrawn within two years and at the time of the
report four foreign agencies remained to compete with "ten
large Canton, Swatow and Chinchew Hongs." The Southern Chinese,
active collaborators in the forties and fifties, were emerging
as strong competitors, particularly on the Yangtze and in the
North. The Newchwang hongs spent Tls. 400,000 annually to
charter foreign-owned vessels as carriers of their merchandise
to and from Shanghai, thereby cutting out the foreign middleman;
through their industry and natural advantages "they engrossed
the business of the port." Their superiority was also attributed
to the fact that Chinese traders dealing with large hongs were,
as local inhabitants familiar with the Liaotung hinterland, able
to judge the width and capacity of the market for Yangtze produce.
Also long-established Chinese hongs had worked with local dealers
for years before the arrival of foreign firms, and had access
to plentiful capital through the "Mukden Banks" which financed
the export trade in pulse.

These advantages were augmented by the relatively low
overhead borne by Chinese merchants when compared to "the
excessive commissions levied by compradores upon foreign

merchants" and the preference of Chinese dealers in the country
for Chinese hongs at Newchwang. The only hopeful sign for
foreigners at this new port, five years after its opening, was
the growing predominance of foreign shipping, which had begun
to usurp the carrying trade of the port, attracting the custom
of junks plying between Newchwang, the Yangtze, and Southern
ports.[6]

In the same year similar reports of Chinese competition
came from other ports opened by the 1858-1860 treaties and from
three of the original ports. From Tientsin it was reported
that the Chinese piece-goods dealers preferred to buy their
goods at Shanghai through agents or from one of the large hongs,
thus by-passing the foreign importers in their city.[7] At Hankow
the "unsatisfactory tea speculations" of 1863-1864, which had
ruined several foreign firms, were blamed upon compradores
said to have speculated on their own account with their em-
ployers' capital. In consequence, Chinese merchants were
monopolizing tea exports to Shanghai, where they preferred to
sell through their established guilds of brokers rather than
at Hankow. Foreign merchants were again at a disadvantage
because they could not contact original holders and their
overheads were high while "native shippers' charges accounts
are but trifling."[8]

From Amoy it was also reported that "Chinese merchants
transact to a great extent their own business without having
recourse to the foreign merchant or intermediary," and in Amoy
also "they appreciate more and more the advantage of employing
foreign to native craft, and they learn at the same time to
dispense with foreign assistance." Brokerage services, formerly
performed by foreign firms or agencies at the outports were
then within the capability of Chinese merchants and, as trade
expanded, commissions on sales and services reverted to the
Chinese.[9]

Only Shanghai provided an optimistic report in 1865. There the opium-receiving ships, now anchored off the Bund, were doing excellent and regular business. British cotton goods had fallen in price and increased in volume because Chinese were reported to be shifting preference from domestic goods to imported cottons. Yet it is significant that Chinese merchants controlled distribution from Shanghai. The city was described in the report as "still a Mine of Gold," which occasionally "yielded brass." There, at least, the major portion of trade was not expected to gravitate to the Chinese hongs since Westerners had firm links with Western markets, experience, communications facilities, and capital, all advantages which were available to the Chinese at most other trade centers, except Hong Kong.[10]

Although these reports stressed the growth of Chinese competition they also described formal cooperation and joint investment between Chinese and Western merchants. In spite of social and political obstacles, some initial development of joint commercial relations had taken place prior to the Treaty of Tientsin and the Convention of Peking. The limited, but definite, interdependence, resulting from essential functions performed by Chinese within Western trading firms, had extended to joint investment in opium and in exports, as well as to the shipping of Chinese-owned goods in foreign vessels on the coast. Western firms at Canton, Hong Kong, and Shanghai had made loans to Chinese merchants and hongs connected with the rapidly-expanding export trade, partly to guarantee a good selection of first crop teas and partly to encourage Chinese investment in export shipments.

In 1848 Jardine's made loans totaling $370,000 to Cantonese merchants in Shanghai at interest rates "just below those prevailing among the Chinese bankers."[11] Less wealthy Western firms, engaged in joint-account business with Chinese banks,

would borrow capital from them or from Chinese merchants
guaranteed by them. Chinese banks also advanced funds to
Western firms which had no London affiliates or lacked
credits with Anglo-Indian banks, thereby enabling them to
finance opium purchases and meet the cost of shipment by
Peninsular and Oriental steamers.[12] Some groups of Chinese
merchants were forced into the opium trade when teas could
be paid for in no other way. Such obligatory cooperation was
only one kind of trade situation in which the majority of
small Western firms were at one time or another dependent
upon the credit of Chinese merchants;[13] Jardine's reported
several times that business was at a standstill in Shanghai
during the fifties because Chinese bankers were alarmed by
reports of the rebellion, or the activity of the "Triads,"
and were calling in their loans to Westerners and Chinese
alike.[14] Chinese were also "large shareholders in foreign
steamship companies,"[15] while some of the principal foreign
mercantile houses invested in Chinese banks.[16] Some foreign
firms were doing business entirely as commission agents for
Chinese merchants.

So successful were many new Chinese firms that the
activity of foreign merchants was being "more and more cir-
cumscribed to supplying the wants of their constituents abroad,"
and at the outports most import business had passed into Chinese
control by 1867.[17] Foreign commercial impact was also diminished
at the outports because foreign-managed steamship companies
provided the transport safety and facility which permitted
Chinese merchants to move their goods from Shanghai and Hong
Kong at economic rates. Tientsin, the best market for British
cotton goods in the late sixties, was lost to foreign firms
because local hongs were able to buy directly from importers at
Shanghai on easy credit terms and ship north in steamships.[18]

The growth of Chinese direct participation in foreign
trade at the outports was paralleled by changes in Hong Kong
and Shanghai where new banks offered cheap capital and encouraged small Western and Chinese traders to join in the
trade as never before.[19] A thriving and wealthy Chinese
community existed in both cities by the late sixties; many
of its members were engaged in commercial transactions "as
extensive as those conducted by Western merchants,"[20] and
had established their own network of branches and agencies
from Canton to Newchwang. Their agents were paramount in the
import trade at Canton, Swatow, and Foochow. Chinese merchants
of Amoy had established new branches throughout Southeast Asia,
dominated the foreign trade of Tientsin, had established ..
close ties with the "most important firms" in shipping and insurance, and had gained ground in the conduct of foreign trade
at Newchang. A customs' report concluded: "It appears certain,
the more the country is opened up, the more trade will fall
into the hands of Native Dealers coming from the old Treaty
Ports."[21]

Better local information available to Chinese, their
greater economy in business, the protection afforded by their
guilds and "natural combines," and the comparative ease with
which they could settle commercial claims through their own
devices, counterbalanced Western assets. These advantages,
common to indigenous merchant groups everywhere, seemed unfair
to many foreigners in China who argued that foreign enterprise
had created the conditions which made possible Chinese gains
at the great centers of Shanghai and Hong Kong as well as at the
outports, gains which they believed had been made through the
use of practices inimical to the spirit of Western enterprise.
Although this view ignored the fact that Chinese merchants would

certainly have competed earlier at the ports if the rebellion had not left initiative with foreigners, it was repeated in official reports.[22]

However, I find no statements of this kind in the private correspondence of Jardine's which from about 1867 concentrates upon the need for cooperation with "native merchants" and refers to the idea that future profits would lie in areas outside Chinese competence.[23] An example of the firm's attitude was its effort to equalize the duties levied upon merchandise shipped via foreign (i.e. Imperial Maritime Customs) and domestic customs; the tariff rates at the domestic customs were lower. The articles specified, in a letter to the Canton Commissioner of Customs, were nankeens (Chinese cotton piece goods), silk, British cotton piece goods, and medicine, all of which were entirely in the hands of Chinese merchants from Shanghai to the interior or northwards, thus: "The question of the assimilation of the tariff without distinction of flag, is one which affects only the mode of conveyance and its results."[24] The firm was concerned with possible discrimination against its shipping, not with taxes upon the movement of goods. This shipping depended upon the custom of Chinese merchants and it was essential to ensure that the Chinese did not revert to junk transport in order to avoid strict customs dues.[25] Discriminatory tariffs might end an association with Chinese merchants from whom they had also begun to enlist capital for joint-stock enterprises.

Thus, in the late sixties the participation of foreigners in China's external trade, as owners or agents in the exchange of goods, had been restricted at all open ports except Shanghai and Hong Kong where they held former gains because of experience and capital. External trade at the outports had become the

preserve of Chinese merchants, as it had been prior to the
rebellion, both in distribution of imports and collection of
exports and their excellent market judgment had reduced profits
for many Western produce agencies to precarious levels. It
had become clear, then, by 1870, that the auxiliary services
of trade were vital to the prosperity of foreigners in China
and that many Western firms had to choose between adaptation
or failure.[26] This process continued during the seventies and
early eighties. The number of foreign firms dependent upon Chinese
aid, either in joint-stock ventures or through technical services
in export, became larger each year as did the number of Chinese
investors in Western-controlled companies.[27] There were also
joint-account commodity speculations between foreign and Chinese
merchants, and joint shares in "purely native institutions, such
as pawnshops and theatres."[28] All reports continued to under-
score gains made by Chinese merchants, their perfect organization,
and their knowledge of local markets. Even in areas where the
advantage was assumed to be with Western enterprise, such as the
establishment of a bean mill to prepare pulse by machinery, the
old Chinese process, preparation by hand with simple tools, had
been found most efficient and economical, given local conditions.[29]

Finally, Chinese bankers in Shanghai, with whom Jardine's
became familiar both as borrower and lender in the seventies,
exemplify the general recovery of domestic commerce; the operations
of the seventy-odd banks with which foreigners had dealings
were described as very large. Their branches in other cities
permitted transfer of funds to Shanghai when interest rates
ruled high and they did not compete among themselves, preferring
cooperation in dealing with foreigners.[30] Although the amounts
involved were not large their growing prominence in Western
accounts of foreign trade testified to new uses of Chinese

capital. The solicitation of this capital for use in foreign-
managed shipping lines, insurance companies, docks, and warehouses had become common practice by 1875.[31]

In sum, Jardine, Matheson and Company reacted to these
developments by an increased emphasis upon the servicing of
trade, and encouragement of cooperation and joint-investment
with the Chinese merchant community between the mid-sixties and
mid-seventies. To some extent, partners were caught up in the
spirit of the T'ung-chih Restoration years, impressed by the
display of Chinese commercial acumen at every port. They assumed
for a time that Chinese merchants might be the natural allies
of Western enterprise in China, once Western firms had moved
into business areas where the Chinese merchant would cooperate
but could not compete without overcoming formidable difficulties.
The capital that Chinese merchants were accumulating in the
ports, and in the centers of the traditional economy, if successfully recruited for expanding trade services would entail further
economic change. Many chance references give the impression
that, for a short time, members of the firm seemed to anticipate
the development of China by a combination of Chinese commercial
capital and Western technical and administrative expertness,
which would be provided by Jardine's and others acting as
managing agents of joint-stock enterprises.

However, these expectations were never part of a general
plan and partners began to realize before 1875 that the development of China would not be achieved by an alliance between the
commercial stratum of the Chinese economy and Western firms in
the treaty ports. After years of increasing joint investment
and at least two abortive attempts to introduce economic innovations in cooperation with Chinese merchants, it became clear that
their hopeful evaluation of the power of the Chinese commercial

class had been incorrect or, at least, premature. Despite the obvious economic strength of a number of Chinese merchant groups and their essential role in foreign trade, it was evident that this position ultimately depended upon official patronage, at best, or official sufferance, at least, while any long-term development, any innovation, in the Chinese economy would rest within the competence of a small number of high officials.

Tseng Kuo-fan had established arsenals and shipyards and had encouraged the study of Western military techniques in the 1860's. Li Hung-chang, Tseng's most intelligent and powerful disciple was "to extend the self-strengthening principle to include the adoption of foreign techniques and methods in transportation, mining, and industry," by means of state control of merchant enterprise.[32] Although self-strengthening was an essentially military response of the Manchu-Chinese bureaucracy to the West in the period after the Treaty of Tientsin, Li Hung-chang called for an economic response to external pressure in a memorial (1872) written in defense of the building of steamships.[33] He recognized that military innovations required expenditure beyond the static revenue of the government and therefore proposed a program of official-directed economic growth:

> Recently Westerners have frequently requested permission to open coal and iron mines in the Chinese interior, pointing out that it is a great pity that China's natural resources cannot be developed by herself. We have heard that now Japan is adopting Western methods of opening coal and iron mines to gain a great profit, and this has also helped her shipbuilding and machinery....If we can really make plans to persuade the people, by means of the system of "government-supervision and merchant management" (kuan-tu shang-pan) to borrow and use foreign machines and foreign methods only,

but not allow foreigners to do the whole job on our behalf,
then these articles of daily necessity, when produced and
processed by proper methods, must have a good market. A
source of profit will naturally be opened. Taking the
surplus funds from the new source we can even use it to
maintain our ships and train our soldiers.[34]

In this way progressive officials meant to enlist capital
and experience for their limited development program. They
hoped to attract support from wealthy compradores and Chinese
merchants in the treaty ports by the offer of positions in the
minor bureaucracy or official connections conferring the status
which remained the ultimate goal of the Chinese businessman,
however successful in commerce. The emergence of this aspect
of self-strengthening checked Jardine, Matheson and Company
plans for the organization of several joint-stock companies in
which Chinese capital would be directed by Western managers to
the inauguration of railroads, mines and industries.

As it became clear during the seventies that the most
powerful Chinese merchants would accept official status and
invest in government-controlled enterprises such as the China
Merchants Steam Navigation Company and the Kaiping Mines, Jardine's
sought another policy, one which would allow them to participate
in kuan-tu shang-pan enterprises by cooperating with their official
sponsors and supervisors.

Chapter IV

COOPERATION WITH THE BUREAUCRACY

In the two decades preceding the traumatic shock of
Japan's victory, officially sponsored projects, in connection
with water control, armaments, and proto-industrialization,
continued to emanate from a small number of powerful bureaucrats
who aimed to hire and strictly control the services of both
Chinese and foreign capitalists in achieving their limited ends.
The salient features of the political and economic background
to these efforts were the continued decline in the value of
silver, a steady increase in the volume of China's foreign trade,
and general support of China's independence by foreign powers
in anticipation of the "awakening."[1] Jardine, Matheson and
Company's participation in officially sponsored programs of
economic change constitutes the most interesting function of
its enterprise in nineteenth-century China.

The firm worked consistently to introduce, on government
orders, railways, factories, modern mining, machinery and flood-
control schemes; its partners sought and maintained close relations
with key figures of the Ch'ing bureaucracy, Li Hung-chang, Tseng
Chi-tse, Chang Chih-tung, Liu Ming-ch'uan, Sheng Hsuan-huai, their
agents, and the court officials of the Nei-wu-fu (Imperial household). The partial record of this interaction reveals the role
played by Western enterprise within the disintegrating order of the
late Ch'ing, a role founded upon an acceptance of government
control over the economy. On the basis of Jardine's experience,
it is evident that large Western firms were not challenging
the bureaucracy nor were they risking capital in support of
Chinese bankers and merchants in an effort to "Westernize" a

sector of the internal economy. Rather, they were similar to
chonin in Japan's early economic development, seeking cooperation with bureaucratic power in order to share in the profits
accruing to the development process.

In playing a variation on the kuan-tu shang-pan program,
seeking official support for its joint-stock proposals or the
agency of official projects, the firm tried to find a way
around the formidable institutional blocks to economic change.
It is ironic that these efforts may have strengthened a social
and political order which could only, in the end, frustrate the
proper development and use of any modernizing project; each plan
was described by modernizing officials as an antiforeign self-
strengthening measure, curtailing foreign power in China. There
was never a concept of economic growth. Western firms with
capital and influence in London were used by Ch'ing officials
for their own ends and were prevented from initiating programs
which, if successful, might multiply, "endanger the people's
livelihood," and weaken bureacratic power.

Li Hung-chang and his group, and a few other people in the
bureaucracy, believed in Chung-hsüeh wei t'i, Hsi hsüeh wei yung
(Chinese learning for basic principles, Western learning for practical
use), two decades before its explicit formulation, using Western
capital and techniques to preserve the traditional order as they
understood it. Even such controlled use of foreign enterprise
had been dictated by necessity rather than by choice. The experience of the China Merchants Steam Navigation Company showed
that the kuan-tu shang-pan formula did not sufficiently attract
Chinese capital, traditionally wary of exposure to official
attention of any sort. The failure of domestic capital to
enlist under official direction compelled the progressive
factions to risk controlled use of foreign capital and foreign
expertness. In Jardine's experience there is always evident

official determination to prevent foreigners from gaining control
of any development scheme, which would defeat its purpose and
expose official-sponsors to the attacks of conservatives within
the bureaucracy.

It followed then that just as the early seventies had
been a watershed in the business history of large Western firms
in China, so the eighties became the years in which these firms
were most willing, for their own reasons, to work with the
Chinese officials who would accept foreign help in the building
of communications to begin the transformation of the old economy.
A new policy had become explicit by 1875. By lending money
for administrative and other essentially non-productive purposes
(i.e military loans) the firm expected to place itself with
Li Hung-chang, and a few others, as the agent through whom the
Chinese government might initiate and supply its further projects. Partners interpreted the early self-strengthening
efforts, the arsenals and steamships, as harbingers of China's
industrialization and of future economic development so vast--
in provision of communications and manufacturing equipment--
that it would dwarf all previous industrial programs. For the
Western agent "on the ground," experienced and favored by Chinese
officials, it was expected that such a program would provide
excellent profits over several decades.[2]

It is clear, however, that Western merchants in China
did not understand how radically different official intentions
were from their own, though Jardine, Matheson and Company
had frequent opportunities to study evidence of this difference.
Not even defeat in the French War, 1883-1884, awakened the
majority of the bureaucracy to the need for basic economic
change. Indeed the eagerness of some may have abated because
of corruption in the management of kuan-tu shang-pan enterprises, badly-administered military projects, and the persistent

conservatism of the majority of court and provincial officials.[3]
Thus official Chinese response to the more ambitious efforts of
Western capitalism in China continued to vary from the cautious
self-strengthening of a small number of high officials to deep
suspicion of all economic innovation on the part of the great
majority of the scholar-official gentry class. Tseng Kuo-fan's
earlier objection to railways, which were vital to modernization
(he believed they were certain to upset China's traditional
economic balance while destroying the livelihood of many
thousands) continued to sum up the attitude of most officials,
central and provincial, until the end of the dynasty.[4]

The archive shows that Jardine, Matheson and Company
were prepared to offer industrial and financial schemes and
to work for the day when the opposition of the conservatives
would be destroyed by the evidence of great benefits. This
willingness to serve rather than to oppose the bureaucracy
directly reached its high point in the decade preceding the
Sino-Japanese War although the great surge of industrial and
financial enterprise, regarded as imminent each year, had
not resulted in many concrete projects before 1895. Private
letters show that the firm was rarely discouraged; F.B.
Johnson's advocacy of "keeping ourselves to the front in any
communications on fiscal arrangements or enterprises taking
place between Chinese authorities and foreigners" guided policy
until 1895. Partners hoped for a China developing commercially
and industrially along Japanese lines, with over-all direction
in government hands while Western firms acted as suppliers of
capital, materials, and skills.

The daily record of Jardine's business with and on behalf
of Chinese officials is extraordinarily varied, but a clear

pattern does emerge. Railway contracts, for financing and supplying of material, seem to have been the ultimate aim while loans, however large and profitable, were regarded as a means of obtaining leverage with those officials with whom the gift of railway contracts was supposed to rest. Second only to railways were loans offered for general engineering work, particularly the repair of the Yellow River flood-control system, the fortification of Port Arthur, and the provision of materials for all engineering work. The sale of armaments, including torpedo boats, followed these larger activities.[5]

Shanghai, Tientsin, and Peking remained the geographic centers of the firm's relations with officials in the eighties and nineties. The important negotiators for Jardine's were the Keswick brothers, James and William, heads in Shanghai and Hong Kong respectively, F.B. Johnson, Herman Mandl, agent-engineer, Alexander Michie, special agent, Gustav Detring, advisor to Li Hung-chang, and James Morrison, the firm's railway engineer. In the eighties Jardine, Matheson and Company's office at Tientsin began to coordinate all the firm's business on behalf of the Chinese government, direct-ing negotiations at Peking and maintaining daily contact with Li Hung-chang's yamen, the center of all development plans for decades.

Loans to Ch'ing officials were, then, a primary instrument in securing cooperation. There is no reason to doubt that the firm had followed in its early days of opium smuggling what James Matheson described as the East India Company's policy of distributing annually £150,000 "among the Emperor's mother and a quadrille of other old ladies...."[6] Certainly, in the fifties and sixties, when the rebellion had diminished all government revenue, either by destroying its agricultural basis or by appropriating the yield of several central provinces, many provincial officials, particularly in the South, were desperate for funds with which to maintain government operations and meet the demands of military levies.[7] In 1858 the Kwangtung provincial government accused Jardine, Matheson and Company's compradore Wu (Pai-chun) of being a traitor and required him to lend Tls. 320,000 at 7.2 per cent per annum, considerably below the prevailing rate of interest in the Chinese economy.[8] Jardine's, on its own account, made at least two small provincial loans to beleagured officials between 1860 and 1865: "we are increasing the loan to the Hankow authorities to Tls. 100,000 at 2 per cent per month. The security for its repayment, Customs Bonds, is good."[9]

Thus there was no sudden shift in the firm's relations with Chinese officials during the watershed period of the early seventies. There was rather an intensification of old policies for definite aims with capital. Having reverted to the stricter practices of an agency house operating on commission and no longer investing large amounts of their own capital in opium, China exports, or in British exports to China, members of the firm were free to emphasize their inherent capacity as managers and financial brokers.

In 1867, after many years of minor loans to officials and to Chinese merchants, the firm was involved in the first sizeable loan to the imperial government, a loan guaranteed by the customs revenue. Robert Hart, the new inspector-general, played a key role.[10] The object of the loan was to provide funds for Tso Tsung-tang's campaign against Moslem rebels in the northwest, the first of a series devoted to the same purpose. Hu Kuang-yung had been delegated to arrange these loans with certain foreign merchants in Shanghai, among them Jardine's, and of the amount required, Tls. 1,200,000 (£400,000) Jardine's

subscribed £200,000; the rest was raised from other Shanghai
firms. Bonds were endorsed by the governors-general and
governors of the related provinces, registered with the Imperial
Maritime Customs, and signed by the commissioner of customs.
Repayment was thus guaranteed out of the customs revenue if
money from the provinces did not arrive on time. The loan,
made in April, 1867, at 15 per cent, provided in its terms a
model for future business with the Chinese government since by
introducing the customs revenue it opened new financial possi-
bilities for merchants willing to act on such security.[11]

Another Northwest Campaign loan, negotiated late in 1867
and signed January 9, 1868, did not attract Jardine's because
the greater part of their funds were "at this time, invested
in good drug," but Hu had no difficulty in again raising
Tls. 1,000,000 at Shanghai and the firm resolved "to be ready
at the next opportunity."[12]

Peking did not authorize further provincial loans until
1874 when money was needed again to finance military operations
in connection with the Liu-ch'iu affair and in the northwest.
Hu Kuang-yung approached Jardine's through their former compradore, Aleet, for Tls. 3,000,000. The firm declined the whole
amount but offered one million quickly if customs security were
provided. Assurance was then given that bonds would be issued
by the customs at Shanghai, Canton and Chinkiang, each for
Tls, 1,000,000, that they would be endorsed by the governors-
general and governors, and that one-sixth of the total would
be returned at the end of every sixth month; the full amount
would be returned within three years, and annual interest would
be 10.5 per cent. On these terms Jardine's agreed to deliver
Tls. 1,000,000 to Hu on April 6, 1875.[13] The firm was satisifed
with this business both as an investment and as an aid to "a

position of influence" with the government, but Matheson and
Company expressed scepticism about the value of customs bonds
and notified Jardine's of their reluctance to participate in a
loan being sought in September, 1876.[14] The subject of loans
was dropped for several months during which the firm was concerned
with a myriad of normal business activities, particularly in
connection with silk (whose value and volume as an export was
then approaching its pre-1895 zenith)[15] until March, 1877, when
a request was submitted to several Western firms and The Hong
Kong and Shanghai Bank for another loan:

> The following is the offer submitted. Tls. 5,000,000
> for ten years, with Customs security guaranteed by the
> Government. If issued on a sycee basis 10% will be the
> rate of interest on a sterling basis, 8%. I believe
> Butterfield and Swire are desirous of obtaining it with
> the object of floating it in Liverpool.[16]

Competition among Western firms able to deal with such large
loans was naturally severe, especially among those who expected
a specific loan to lead to more important business. Later the
firm secured the loan as a joint venture with the Hong Kong and
Shanghai Bank:

> The Chinese Government have with us in conjunction with
> the Hongkong and Shanghai Bank, arranged a loan of
> Tls. 5,000,000 Haikwan (Customs) Sycee, equal to £1,004,000
> for seven years, repayment being arranged half-yearly in
> fourteen equal installments. One half the amount will be
> paid to the Chinese on 1 September and the balance by
> installments extending into January. The Bank undertakes to
> finance the entire amount and the payment of so large a
> sum in Silver will help our exchange in London, keeping
> it steady, but will not I think cause an advance as the

Bank has already secured Silver in London and San
Francisco to pretty nearly meet their requirements.[17]

Cooperation between the bank and the firm had been
dictated by mutual need rather than policy or preference
(although the senior member of the firm became a director
of the bank in 1877) and the firm continued to regard the
bank as its major competitor in the business of loans and
investments. Jardine's small commercial loans to Chinese firms
were disliked by the bank as much as their transfer of loan
business to London when they failed to raise capital in the
treaty ports.

During 1878 Hu Kuang-yung approached the bank for
another Tls. 2,000,000 loan made necessary by the severe
financial strain of the Moslem Rebellion (Tso Tsung-tang had
recently captured Kashkar, Sinkiang). Jardine's followed
the course of negotiations; they were particularly interested
in the rumor that the imperial edict might not be issued
because conservative officials were afraid of incurring further
debts to foreigners,[18] and that the Chinese government would
forfeit its bargain money, Tls. 100,000, to the Hong Kong Bank.
However, the edict was finally granted and the loan made
late in 1878, issued in Shanghai at 8 per cent and listed on
the Hong Kong share market. In September, 1879, Jardine's
invested the credit balance of its China Coast Steam Navigation
Company in bonds of "The Chinese 8% loan of 1878."[19]

The growing financial need of the Chinese government
was evident to all foreign merchants in China by the end
of the seventies but no one could be sure of its extent.
Frank Forbes of Russell and Company visited Li Hung-chang's
yamen several times in October, 1879, and offered to pay the
Chinese government the Tls. 2,000,000 owed to it by the China

Merchants Steam Navigation Company (Russell and Company had sold their Yangtze fleet to the China Merchants Steam Navigation Company in 1877), in return for management of the Chinese company, whose property would also stand as security for the loan.[20] Li Hung-chang was reported to have refused the offer only after careful consideration. Later it was rumored that the proposal was objected to by official shareholders, from which Jardine's concluded that the financial needs of the Chinese government were, as given out, directly related to the Moslem Rebellion or famine relief (the great drought famine, 1878-1879) and not to a more profound internal crisis, as some in the treaty ports had believed.[21]

A final Moslem campaign loan was sought by the Chinese government in 1881. Tls. 4,400,000 was asked of the bank, again through Hu to whom the firm immediately protested that it had not been offered an opportunity to participate; he replied that Jardine's would certainly be given an option on the next loan which, he suggested, would be sought within a short time.[22]

By the early eighties loan fever was rampant, especially in relation to railways. The firm tried to put railway schemes before Li Hung-chang several times; when the building of a short (seven-mile) line at the Kaiping Mines during 1880-1881 encouraged new expectations,[23] Matheson and Company sent their terms:

> If the Imperial Government seriously contemplated
> the construction of railways in the Empire the considera-
> tion of financial questions therewith is inevitable,
> and it is in regard thereto that we are now stating the
> conditions upon which we would undertake to float an
> Imperial Loan in London, i.e. 95 net price for every
> 100 £, 7% interest, 1% sinking Fund.[24]

During the summer of 1881 there was also a great
deal of correspondence on railways and loans between the
Hong Kong and Shanghai offices and between both and London.
James Morrison had discussed the firm's "secret terms" with
Jardine's Tientsin agent, who felt that they were such "as
it would be useless to lay before the proper authorities"
at that time.[25] However, the Tientsin agent wrote that he
had long cultivated close relations with Gustav Detring,
commissioner of customs in Tientsin and Li Hung-chang's
closest Western adviser: "and I can confidently say that
any proposal of mine would be submitted to the Viceroy quite
confidentially and without any German firms learning anything
whatever on the subject. There has been serious (Chinese)
opposition to railways but the matter may turn up again at
any moment, and it is for this reason that I want to place
Mr. Detring in possession of full details so that he may
bring them forward whenever the opportune moment arrives."[26]

J. Keswick promised to furnish him with a better,
more definite set of terms which he could discuss with Detring
and he began to draw up terms to which "our London friends"
(Matheson and Company) might acquiesce. In outlining these to
London, he confessed that the firm had no definite information
regarding railways and wanted clear terms at that time simply
in order to be prepared.[27]

In an effort to get more definite information Morrison
was sent to Peking where he was to try to see Tso Tsung-tang,
returned triumphant from the West to Peking for his brief time
as member of the Grand Council and of the Tsungli Yamen.
Jardine's effort to discuss railways with him shows a shrewd
assessment of the disposition of power within the imperial
government, if not of Tso's character. The interview was refused

on the grounds that Tso was too busy and ill, both statements
being most likely true.[28] Morrison returned to Tientsin
where, through Detring, he had two short interviews with Li
in August, 1881; these were described as "satisfactory."[29]
Li mentioned a series of possible short-period loans which
might be needed on brief notice and he implied "that those
who accommodated the Chinese Government in this way would be
well placed for future business."[30] Keswick had authorized
his Tientsin agent to offer a loan up to Tls. 2,000,000, at
9 per cent per annum for one year, and 8 1/2 per cent per
annum for two years or more, in order "to give us a fair chance
of making a beginning with the Chinese authorities."[31]

In July negotiations were also started with the
Shanghai manager of the Comptoir et D'Escompte Bank, in which
J. Keswick offered the French bank a half interest in any
loan negotiated by them. (He had stressed the point that in
combination the two firms would be better able to compete
against the Hong Kong and Shanghai Bank.) Keswick said:

> This afternoon I had a long interview with Mr.
> Hardcastle regarding loans to the Chinese Government.
> We will go into business with them on joint account for
> loans that may be floated here or in Europe. At present,
> with an Imperial Edict, we could make a fair profit
> out of a loan for one or two years but nothing will now
> be done at Tientsin until everything is properly arranged.[32]

In the same week Morrison wrote from Tientsin that his second
interview with Li confirmed the likelihood that a big loan
would be asked of Jardine's very soon: "I think it is
fortunate that we have agreed to go in with the Comptoir."[33]

A clear statement of the firm's lack of a very large
amount of surplus capital in China came out of the Comptoir

negotiations. Its function in loan negotiations was described
as that of "mere agent," with Matheson and Company providing
the money to match the Comptoir and Jardine's acting only as
the former's agents: "If Matheson and Company are not prepared to put us in this position, I think we may leave loans
alone."[34] However, the London firm telegraphed within the
week that they would be prepared to work with the Comptoir
on joint-account if the Chinese government offered "Treasury
Bonds" (bonds guaranteed by the Hupu or Board of Revenue)
or Imperial Maritime Customs revenue bonds as security.[35]
Jardine's was heartened by such prompt support, only to have
it withdrawn before a month had passed; Matheson and Company
explained that they could not be interested in loan business
at that time because of other commitments and Sir Robert
Jardine, senior partner of Matheson and Company, suggested
that Jardine's seek a closer understanding with the Hong
Kong and Shanghai Bank before seeking further loan business.
Paterson wrote: "Disappointed to learn that Matheson and
Company decline China loans after all and think they must be
doing so under some misconception. It is very annoying to
find that we have probably had all our trouble for nothing."[36]

A clearer example of Matheson and Company's cautious
attitude came in 1883. Sir Robert Jardine responded to yet
another Jardine, Matheson proposal that his firm could not
afford to put an estimated $825,000 ($500,000 of it in a loan
requested by the China Merchants at 8 per cent--$325,000 as
the price of the "Ningpo Wharf") "in so permanent an investment and on behalf of a Chinese Company." He pointed out that
"we have large necessary investments which will give us an
assured and good return here (London) and elsewhere, devoid
of such risk."[37] His letter is an explicit restatement of

Jardine, Matheson and Company's agency character and of Matheson and Company's desire to avoid long-term investment of its capital (i.e Jardine, Matheson and Company's liquid assets also) in China, even when such investment was intended to secure a valuable agency. It also reflects a Western businessman's distrust of Chinese-controlled enterprise.

In September it was reported that Li Hung-chang could have authority to establish railways providing that he consent to bribe one or two high officials in Peking.[38] More concrete was the news that Li had sent one of his deputies to Shanghai to see if two well-known silk merchants (Koo Feng-sing and Tah Sun) would agree to help in the establishment of a Chinese company which would construct a railway between Tientsin and Peking.[39] In this instance Jardine's drew upon close associations formed through loans and joint-account business with prominent Chinese at Shanghai. When Tah Sun replied to Li's request by saying that he would form such a company under certain conditions,[40] the firm assured him that it would handle all financial matters on his behalf and would advance, on the security of the line, whatever money was required: "I do not know if it will come to anything, but, if it does, through Tah Sun, we shall, I think, have the building of it."[41] Nothing came of this plan, yet the firm's enthusiasm for official projects, and for the development of modern communications was not dampened as is clear in the record of their activity after the Sino-French War.

The war's further exposure of Western aggressiveness brought an increased awareness of the need for self-strengthening military power and a growing realization that military power was an adjunct of industrial power, that arsenals and shipyards called for a wide range of supporting industrial and communications projects.

The creation of the Hai-chun Yamen or Naval Office in October 1885 (Prince Ch'un, Controller; Li Hung-chang and Prince Ch'ing, Associate Controllers), first of many new official military projects, was a direct result.[42]

The war had been at first deplored by the firm on the ground that it would disturb trade, but later comment favored strong French pressure on Peking as likely to hasten favorable change.[43] During the war, James Keswick, as chairman of the Shanghai Chamber of Commerce, had asked F.B. Johnson, then in London, to cooperate with the London Chamber of Commerce in working to procure the intervention of neutral powers in order to arrange a settlement or extract a pledge from the French that they would not attack Shanghai.[44] Johnson replied that they had been told by the Foreign Office that "it would be most impolitic to seek to extract from the French Government any public declaration which would restrict their freedom in the conduct of the war." He had also suggested a public meeting which would advise limiting the area of hostilities. However, Lord Granville, the foreign secretary, replied so coldly that the idea was dropped.[45] After the French had destroyed the Foochow arsenal and it had become evident that they did not intend to attack Shanghai, Johnson wrote to Philip Currie, then in charge of the China department of the Foreign Office, suggesting that Lord Granville consider the French victory an opportune time to tender the good offices of the British government in order to better relations. Granville replied: "Tell Mr. Johnson that I do not see any way to interfere with good effect."[46] In time Johnson also doubted the value of neutral intervention and wrote : "Whatever the merits or demerits of the French claim (to indemnity in the Fournier Treaty) it is certainly not in the

interest of foreigners that the Chinese who also have un-
questionably pursued a very devious policy should be encouraged
to resist or should come off victorious."[47]

The Shanghai Chamber agreed that Chinese success,
diplomatic or military, would be a calamity to China and
foreign powers alike. Many seem to have expected an "awakened
China," shocked into a greater appreciation of Western-type
development by military defeat and diplomatic humiliation.

The financial strain of the war was evident to all;
apart from small loans to the China Merchants, to Li Hung-
chang and to various provincial officials there were seven
major loans contracted by the Chinese government during the
war.[48] One of these, the £1,500,000 loan floated by Baring
Brothers in London, had been negotiated by Jardine's with
Li Hung-chang and the firm was also involved to some extent
in the negotiations for each of five Hong Kong and Shanghai
Bank loans made in 1884-1885.[49] From that time Jardine's
cooperated almost continuously with the bank when seeking
government business and many informal agreements were made
limiting the respective spheres of both in dealing with the
Chinese government.[50] The head of the bank supplied the firm
with information gathered through its banking business on
behalf of Chinese officials, merchants, and banks in Hong Kong
and Shanghai, and the firm shared similar commercial intelligence.

Cooperation was difficult because of the commanding
position of Li Hung-chang, whose numerous agents, foreign and
Chinese, suggested and arranged contracts and loans in private
personal meetings so that a promised contract might result in
the bank and the firm unwittingly working against each other.[51]
An example of their cooperation may be seen in April, 1884,
just after French troops had engaged Chinese on the Annam border

and had forced a divided Chinese government to seek negotiations.
When the firm learned that the governor of Fukien required
Tls. 2,000,000 urgently, probably to prepare coastal defenses,
a member wrote: "I have no doubt we can manage through
Matheson and Company to negotiate it in Europe but the conditions
may be difficult to arrange for there is not silver out here
with which to make the large payments required. The terms
would necessarily include exchange and other items probably
requiring much explanation."[52] However, Matheson and Company
again insisted that any loan be issued under imperial sanction
in sterling on the London market, thereby raising so many
difficulties that the Hong Kong and Shanghai Bank finally made
the loan at Jardine's request.[53]

In 1885 a larger and much more important loan was
under discussion. Through Michie the Shen Chi Ying (Peking
Field Force) directed by Prince Ch'un (I-huan), had applied
for Tls. 6,000,000 (£1,500,000), part of which "would be used
for military purposes but part also to construct railways and
develop mines."[54] After considerable negotiation Matheson
and Company agreed to raise the entire amount in London with
Maritime Customs bonds offered as security; interest of 10
per cent was to be repaid in Shanghai through the taotai,
running regularly and quarterly on the whole amount until
repayments of principal began.[55] Tls. 2,500,000 of the loan
was paid to Li Hung-chang at Tientsin in August, the remaining
being transferred to Peking in sycee during the same month.
There, the Shen Chi Ying gave Michie receipts for the sterling
equivalent of the silver delivered.

Never before had a department of the imperial government been in such heavy debt to foreign creditors except for

war indemnities. Jardine's hopes of Chinese government
business were so high that Mandl was instructed to stay in
constant attendance upon Li Hung-chang and Gustav Detring.
Michie was encouraged to be more active in Peking, and
Matheson and Company were asked if they could organize a
financial syndicate in London which would handle Chinese railway loans. They replied that it would be difficult to create
a syndicate at that time since "political complications on
the continent are increasing" and recommended continued cooperation with the Hong Kong and Shanghai Bank in the China
capital market. Keswick commented:

> In view of the indication of this message and my
> own knowledge of Matheson and Company's indisposition to
> give us financial assistance we must either strengthen
> ourselves by combinations here, and lessen the opposition
> to business coming to us, or else in a very great measure
> retire from making efforts to secure official business.[56]

A remarkable feature of Jardine, Matheson and Company's reaction
to what they believed to be the economic opportunities of late
Ch'ing China was the firm's persistence in government business
although their major associate often refused cooperation and
insisted upon maximum security of investment. The atmosphere
of China markets imparted a sense of great, profitable changes
which could not be conveyed intact to London.

Undaunted by Matheson and Company's caution, much
attention focused upon the many railway and loan proposals
which came up in the summer and autumn of 1885. James Morrison
visited Peking and Tientsin to discuss a Peking-Tientsin railway
and the extension of the short Kaiping mine railway to Pehtang.
Mandl established a "native agency" at Tientsin to recruit

Chinese capital and solicit orders for telegraph equipment
from provincial authorities,[57] and Alexander Michie as usual,
reported progress "at the Palace."[58]   The firm had not lost
confidence in the plans of progressive officials or in their
ultimate triumph.

Chapter V

THE FIRM AS SPECIAL AGENT TO THE CHINESE GOVERNMENT

Jardine, Matheson and Company's confidence in a government-directed program of economic development for China is best
illustrated in the record of meetings between members of the firm
and Li Hung-chang or his agents. Mining enterprise provides a
useful example of the nature of these relations. Since the 1870's
the firm had employed mining engineers to test and report on
potential sites in China, Malaya, and Korea with the intention of
organizing joint-stock companies to develop the most promising
locations.

In the autumn of 1885, James Keswick saw Li Hung-chang
several times in order to discuss the development of sites in
China. During one of these interviews Li proposed that Jardine's
become general manager of the Kaiping Mines, blaming incompetent
management for what he described as "heavy losses." The chief
engineer of the Kaiping, Claude Kinder, had taken Keswick over
the mine and told him that 600 tons per day (some 200,000 tons
annually) could be mined and profitably sold.[1] Kinder supported
full Jardine control of the enterprise while warning that there
would be considerable opposition to such control and to the reforms which Keswick envisaged. He believed that Mr. Wang, Tientsin
manager of the China Merchants was "most hostile to any control
being exercised by foreigners over undertakings in China which
are Chinese" and that Wang had gone to Peking in order to warn
high officials of Jardine's attempts to gain control of the
enterprise.[2]

Michie, acting for the firm in Tientsin and Peking, was
asked to report on Wang's mission, to do whatever possible to

neutralize its effects and to remind officials that Jardine, Matheson and Company would not advance money on behalf of the Kaiping Mines or any railway company without official recognition and support though such support was not to mean any form of control. The firm required full control of the property which would be its responsibility to manage and asked the Chinese government to guarantee loans only, while leaving management and supervision to the firm.[3]

Gustav Detring, Li's adviser, also favored Jardine control of the Kaiping Mines; he assisted at interviews with Li in which Keswick explained his intentions. During one interview Li seemed to sanction Jardine, Matheson and Company's construction of the proposed Taku-Tientsin railway extension yet he promised nothing definite nor did he approve their Kaiping plans.[4] Tong King-sing, the firm's former compradore, had agreed in November to send a petition to Li supporting the firm's request for full control, but he also wrote later that the viceroy was determined to stop foreign interests from securing unsupervised management of the mines. Li had given Keswick the opposite impression during their several interviews. Even if Tong was right, Keswick argued that a managing agent would be required in the near future: "I believe the position of things is hopelessly bad with Kaiping and that this fact is dawning upon the Viceroy."[5]

Li had also discussed his plans for the development of coal and iron mines in Shansi, and the construction of a railroad to connect Shansi with Tientsin. Keswick had promised that Morrison would spend the winter in the province to investigate its mining potential and a good railway route: "It would be the best means by which we would become the pioneer company of railways on a large scale in China."[6] These hopeful discussions of mining projects seemed to prefigure once again substantial changes in China, though Keswick was aware of opposition within the Chinese government and he knew that much depended upon Li's personal power.[7]

Opposition from within the bureaucracy did defeat the firm's effort to secure general managership of the Kaiping Mines, though Keswick's interviews with Li eventually resulted in Michie's negotiation of a loan (Tls. 750,000) to the Kaiping administration in return for which Jardine, Matheson was given the Kaiping agency in Shanghai.[8] Within six months, in the course of other Chinese government business, the firm learned that its attempt to secure control of the Kaiping Mines had made a number of officials in Li's entourage and in Peking intensely suspicious of the proposals. A tender made by the firm for the supply of steel rails to the Kaiping railway extension failed in favor of the German syndicate, and was "undoubtedly another consequence of this suspicion."

Interest in China's mineral potential revived again in the spring of 1887, part of the general atmosphere of "awakening" which seemed to pervade those months. Henderson, a mining engineer resident in Tientsin, described several potential sites and asked the firm's support.[9] Keswick replied that the firm was very willing to be concerned in the development of mines as agents on commission but not in such a way that they would expend large sums which might not be recovered; he repeated the view expressed at the time of their Korean mining venture (see Appendix C), that they wished to act on behalf of the imperial or a provincial government. His letter conceded that the Chinese government was properly reluctant to permit foreign control of mining enterprise. What he hoped to see was a Chinese organization which would hire Jardine, Matheson as financial and managing agents.[10] Keswick was convinced that the Chinese public would not invest in a company

unless it was secure from official interference.[11] Yet what
he had in mind as an alternative to entirely Chinese joint-
stock enterprises was an arrangement certain to be resisted
by the entire official class and its compradore or merchant-
official associates. His justified indictment of the kuan-tu
shang-pan enterprises led him to misjudge their purpose, which
was to retain official control over the economy rather than
to encourage economic development as a good in itself.[12]

Keswick did not see the contradiction in believing
that official permission would be granted to tap Chinese capital
for productive enterprises which would have Western management and assure Chinese investors protection from official control and exaction. He wrote to Henderson:

> If the Chinese government would grant a concession to
> a native organization with which our name was associated
> we could raise the capital in China to work mines on a
> great scale. I would propose that the concern should be
> a National one and be kept in touch with the Government
> through a Board of Mines or some such Department.[13]

In his July, 1887, talks with Li Hung-chang, Keswick
explained these ideas. Li referred briefly to great difficulties, then displayed specimens of silver from Jehol and asked
if Jardine's would lend Tls. 200,000 for the development of
the mines from which it came. Pragmatically accepting Li's
disinterest in wider plans, Keswick agreed to the loan in
return for the receipt of orders for mining machinery, because
he hoped that the development of Jehol meant the beginning
of a mining industry.[14] However, as in other areas of promising
economic development, Li offered no further opportunities in
mining.

A further example of the firm's effort to act as agent
for the Chinese government was the work of Alexander Michie.
He stood at the center of its network of personal contacts with
the bureaucracy and sought to influence Chinese official opinion
in favor of Jardine, Matheson and Company's objectives. To
accomplish this he traveled between Peking and Tientsin, meeting
officials, managing Jardine's Tung Yuen private bank at both
places, editing two Tientsin newspapers, The Chinese Times and
Shih pao, besides a host of other lesser duties. His special
agent techniques at Peking and Tientsin throw some light on the
methods used by Western firms to encourage officials to accept
the plans of a Western firm for China's development.

When the Chinese government asked in January, 1886, to
delay payment of the 10 per cent charge, Tls. 150,000, on the
Shen Chi Ying loan, Michie telegraphed from Peking advising
the firm to have Matheson and Company bring Tseng Chi-tse,
Chinese Minister in London, to apply pressure in Peking. Keswick
was strongly opposed to this idea: "It does not seem politic
at all to say anything about the matter in London where, were
it known for an instant that there was a hitch in the payment
of interest, any number of exaggerated reports might get
abroad."[15]

China's credit rating in London was to be protected
and their own reputation as brokers guarded. Before the end of
the month Michie had reached an agreement by which interest
was closed to October 31, 1885, on the whole loan so that future
payments would be due quarterly and cover the entire Tls. 150,000.
He blamed the delay in payment upon Russell and Company and
Hong Kong Bank employees in Peking, accusing them of attempting
to discredit the firm by assuring high officials that they
were being overcharged. He also spoke of "evil intrigues" against

the firm on the part of Chinese in Peking who said that China had been overcharged for the Shen Chi Ying loan and that Jardine, Matheson was responsible. One of Michie's major tasks was to quiet these rumors.[16]

In the next month he was negotiating on the details of the prime contract for the fortification of Port Arthur, Li Hung-chang's current self-strengthening project.[17] In his letters he tried to be specific about the bureaucratic and personal factions surrounding Li Hung-chang, but even at the center of negotiations between Chinese officials and Western firms it was not always possible to sort out general purposes. Michie's letters are full of speculation about official intentions though he was close enough to some officials to convey their messages to each other in his own correspondence.[18]

He also provided the Shanghai office with timely information about the activity of others involved in government business:

> The American Minister is on a tour of the ports and is accompanied as far as Shanghai by the "railway" General Wilson. I also call your attention to Ristelhuber's long stay in Shanghai as he is a great commercial schemer and much allied to our friend Sheng the Slippery. [Sheng Hsuan-huai] I also tell you that the Seventh Prince [Prince Ch'un] will leave Peking on 16 May for Tientsin, Port Arthur and Shanghai, the latter part of the program being very important if true.[19]

Keswick replied that he would see the American Minister and that Mandl was trying to discover if Ristelhuber, representing a French syndicate, and Sheng had met.[20] Keswick also suggested that Michie write a newspaper article about Prince Ch'un's projected visit in order to "direct public feeling in the right way."[21]

Michie also gave advice on how to negotiate with Chinese officials. He told Keswick not to regret that he had to negotiate with local officials in Shanghai about payment of interest on the Shen Chi Ying loan because local officials could provide useful business information. And in the same letter he advised that the British consul in Shanghai be kept out of the negotiations: "I think the Chinese officials are scared of Consuls."[22]

All of Michie's personal representations were difficult to arrange because he could not speak Chinese, thus he continually urged the firm to train and recruit Chinese-speaking Europeans for their staff,[23] arguing that expanding business in China would now depend upon negotiations which demanded direct communication and would bypass interested compradores. His advice on this point led to the appointment of two staff members as language students in Peking.[24]

In May Prince Ch'un left Peking for Tientsin as announced, setting off a number of competitive maneuvers in the Shanghai and Tientsin business communities. At Shanghai the firm had just received Tls. 200,000 on fixed deposit at 6 per cent from Sheng Hsuan-huai who had sent a relative to greet the Prince at Tientsin. This man was charged with the task of arguing for Sheng's reinstatement as customs taotai of Tientsin and of furthering Jardine's ambitious plan to become favored agents in all development schemes. James Keswick saw Sheng's relative before his departure "in order to insure that he was free from any animosity" and William Keswick went to Tientsin in expectation that, through Detring, he would see the Prince, controller of the Board of Admiralty, about naval contracts.[25] Every foreign broker at Tientsin in May, 1886, was interested in obtaining contracts for the new navy and the large engineering works required in the fortification of Port Arthur. Michie reported that the French engineers had made some progress.[26]

Keswick arrived on the nineteenth but the Prince,
taking Detring as the only foreigner in his retinue, had
boarded a steamer to travel from Luhshun Kao to Chefoo and
did not return to Taku until the twenty-first.[27] After talking
to Michie and Detring, Keswick did not expect any concrete
results from the visit, though he wrote that "there is a general
impression that we are on the eve of important changes."[28]
In fact, the Prince's tour brought no concrete developments
though he wrote many poems celebrating his reception. Contracts were not negotiated and large plans were not discussed
with him, yet treaty-port opinion remained convinced that a new
era had begun.

Through the summer and autumn of 1886, much Shanghai-
Tientsin correspondence dealt with proposed contracts for
armaments, railways, railway materials, telegraph equipment,
loans, Port Arthur fortifications and Formosa.[29] Michie was
concerned with Port Arthur contracts as part of his arms
business, although initially the fortification had been
entrusted by Li to a French syndicate without contract; it
is not possible to judge whether this was conceived as a shrewd
gesture of political conciliation or was an honest result of
low French bidding. In any case, by July, the French were
reported in trouble at Port Arthur because of "incompetent
staff" and the unexplained fall from favor of their official
allies,[30] thus providing Michie with an opportunity quickly
grasped. Li's yamen was visited daily.[31] It is clear from
these meetings that Li and his group were almost entirely
dependent upon Detring or the many foreign agents around
the yamen to expound the intricacies of weapons technology,
which explains Michie's stress upon the need for competent

technical men from Armstrong. He wrote: "I gather Armstrong's
want to know exactly what kind of torpedo boat the Chinese
require. But that is just what the Chinese do not know themselves," and "If Armstrong will promptly send out a technical
man we can polish off the others. Yet the wisest plan would
be for the four renowned English firms (Armstrong, Thompson's,
Laird's and [illegible]) to coalesce instead of feverishly
competing one against another and I am suggesting to Whittall
[Matheson and Company] to see if he cannot bring that about."[32]

While Michie and Fliche offered Armstrong arms in the
North, Donald Spence, another renowned special agent, was
active in the South negotiating with Liu Ming-ch'uan, the
"progressive" first governor of Formosa. His negotiations concerned the laying of a deep-sea telegraph cable between the
island and the mainland, a steamer to service the cable, and
twelve "fortress guns" for defense of the island so recently
subjected to French attack. The gun contract for Tls. 600,000
had been signed in May, 1886, and since each cannon weighed
43 tons the governor had also inquired about railway equipment
to transport and perhaps permanently carry the guns.[33]   (This
enquiry led to plans for the construction of a railway between
Taipeh and Keelung.) Spence also signed the undersea telegraph
contract with the governor, calling for a cable from Amoy to
Formosa and, in a separate clause, for a "steel steam laying
and repairing tender." Preliminary discussion had taken place
between Spence and Li Tung-en, Liu's secretary, treating the
details of this contract but ranging over proposals for a Formosa
railway system, further telegraph lines, and the financing of
such projects.[34]   The firm offered to lend the governor up to
Tls. 1,000,000 at 8 per cent per annum. Li Tung-en replied
that the governor approved their willingness to help and would
give each plan careful consideration.[35]

Before offering these proposals the firm had consulted with the Hong Kong and Shanghai Bank and had received
an assurance that the "Formosa field should be left to Jardine
Matheson" though warned that in the matter of loans the Germans
and Americans were sending agents to Liu Ming-Ch'uan and would
be active competitors.[36] However Spence's personal favor with
the governor guaranteed Jardine's position and their agency
for Liu's entire development program in the late eighties.[37]
Their position as arms agent to the governor also brought
them the Formosa railway contract in June, 1887. Prior private
loans had been made to Liu's secretaries, Li Tung-en (Tls.
10,000 for three years) and Chang Tsu-ho (Tls. 30,000 for three
years); "Both men will doubtless render other more useful
services." The firm's commission on the railway contract was
not large, prestige being the aim: "...it is one of the biggest
things that has been done in the way of contracts, and, being
for railway materials has a specific importance in the eyes
of the world."[38]

Until conservative pressure forced Liu Ming-ch'uan's
removal from the governorship, his orders for railway materials
and arms were almost entirely channeled through Jardine's
agency, a model situation for those members of the firm who
envisaged a general awakening led by progressive officials,
financed and supplied by willing Western firms.

Perhaps the clearest example of the bureaucracy's
continued ability to use foreign agents with discrimination
came out of the struggle in the eighties to control the Yellow
River, and the linking of this struggle with the fortification
of Port Arthur.

In May 1883 a plan for control of the river, presented
in a memorial by Yu Po-ch'uan, had been accepted by the governor

of Shantung and work had begun, but three years later control
had still not been achieved. Jardine, Matheson and Company then
informed officials that they could succeed where the bureaucracy
had failed. Control of the Yellow River had been under discussion
in the firm's correspondence for several years before the new
floods of the eighties. Morrison had prepared detailed engineering plans when reports indicated that Peking was considering the financial side of an extensive flood-control program.[39]
The firm was asked by the compradore of the North China Insurance
Company if, "should a request come from Prince Ch'un," they
would be able to supply Tls. 5,000,000 or perhaps Tls. 10,000,000
at 6 per cent for the Yellow River Conservancy Fund. While declining to consider such terms, Keswick telegraphed Michie urg-
ing him to keep the firm in view and to make every effort to
forestall alternative proposals on flood control from the French,
the Hong Kong Bank, and the Germans.[40]

Jardine's worked against these powerful competitors in
order to preserve its role as middleman between China and the
resources of the West; the bank's threat was especially severe
because it could finance in China without necessarily calling
on London and because of its contact with many engineering
and manufacturing interests in Europe. Meanwhile, on October
21, Li Hung-chang's secretary announced that a French group
had been awarded the Port Arthur fortification contract amount-
ing to Tls. 1,150,000 worth of materials and supervision. It
appeared then that military plans had taken precedence over
the civil engineering of the river. Cousins, of the firm's
Tientsin office, attributed French success to "lavish but
judicious palm greasing" and lamented the contract as a major
setback to the firm's plans in North China: "it puts an end
to our prospects of further orders at Port Arthur [Michie had

been selling cement and copper to Chinese officials directing the preliminary work] and gives them the pied-a-terre which they have been looking for." He later discovered that the French Syndicate had advanced Tls. 600,000 to Shantung provincial officials through the Tientsin taotai while negotiating for Port Arthur, and he pointed out that loans on favorable terms had been, as Michie argued, an excellent means of influencing official decisions.[41]

Keswick felt that Sheng Hsuan-huai and Li had deliberately misled his agents by allowing them to negotiate minor preliminary contracts at Port Arthur. He asked Michie to write to Sir John Walsham, the British Minister, explaining the dangers of the French victory, its threat to British interests, the manner in which Jardine contracts had been cancelled and the duplicity of Li Hung-chang's entourage: "I hope Sir John may see occasion to drop a word in season at the [Tsungli] Yamen which may make matters increasingly warm for Li Hung-chang."[42] He believed that Li was not immune to pressures from Peking, a belief perhaps justified by the viceroy's subsequent (November 10) assurance to Cousins that the French had won their contract fairly, yet he would give "first consideration" to Jardine's when railway materials were wanted for the proposed Tientsin-Taku railway.[43]

Control of the Yellow River came under consideration again within a year. Correspondence and telegrams between Peking, Tientsin, and Shanghai discussed a major break in Yellow River dikes because of severe floods during the final months of 1887 and into the new year. Li Hung-chang announced through Detring that all expenditure on armaments would be suspended until relief and reconstruction needs had been assessed,[44] thus affecting the firm's negotiations for Wei-hai-wei fortifications. Rumors immediately began to circulate about

possible loans in connection with the floods. Mandl reported
that neither Peking nor the provincial treasuries could cope
with the need; Michie wired that "high officials had inquired
about terms for a loan of six million taels by imperial edict
and covered by customs revenue." Discussion of this loan reached
the stage at which the firm considered the difficulty of issuing
it in silver.

> All that the Chinese authorities would have to do with
> Sterling is to arrange with us what equivalent amount in
> Gold Bonds would be required to be issued to the Public.
> We would pay them the Taels which would constitute the
> loan and hold them free from any claim in respect of the
> Gold Bonds so long as stipulated principal and interest
> payments were regularly paid to us in Silver.[45]

Matheson and Company agreed to 8 per cent as the rate of
interest, anticipating that the loan could be placed at 5
per cent and a certain portion of the margin laid aside annually
to meet possible depreciation in silver.[46]

However, Michie soon reported that Chenfou (Ch'eng
Fu) had raised Tls. 2,000,000, half from the Hong Kong and
Shanghai Bank and the other from sources unkown to his
informants, for relief and rebuilding and he thought a further
loan of Tls. 6,000,000 unlikely. Keswick wired to ask if there
was any chance of a large general loan "to cover the expenses
connected with the Emperor's marriage as well as the cost of
public works needed for the Yellow River." Michie replied that
"the chests of the various treasuries (of Peking) are very
empty." But there was no talk of a large loan.[47]

Mandl then had several interviews at Li Hung-chang's
yamen in which he offered the firm's plan for control of the
river. After several weeks it became clear that officials

willing to accept some foreign financial aid were not willing
to have repairs supervised by foreign contractors. A traditional
function, maintainance of water works, was threatened by
pressing foreign offers to control the river and Li astutely
parried them, in Jardine's case, by promising in May,1888,
that the firm would be sent for if Li Ho-nien and Ch'eng Fu
then in charge, "failed to complete the repair of the breach."[48]
Vincent Smith and "Black" Butler of Russell and Company also
saw Li several times to offer their services "either for Yellow
River control or Manchurian Mines" and the French Syndicate
made frequent proposals.[49] The Hong Kong Bank and Jardine's
were cooperating and Keswick had: "engaged with (The Bank)
to keep in touch with the executive part of the work so as
to keep the French Syndicate out and prevent the Bank from
going past us direct to London engineers and contractors."[50]

In early August, Spence learned from a secretary to
Li that the French had put forward a scheme so comprehensive
that it would involve engineering work along the river for many
years. Keswick commented: "I should think the Chinese Authorities
would fight shy of letting the French Government get a footing
in China under the plea of regulating the Yellow River."[51] Spence
and Morrison were instructed to emphasize the role of the French
government in the French Syndicate and to stress Jardine's
character as a non-governmental private firm.

Another plan, designed to keep the financing of Yellow
River control in Chinese hands, was a national lottery reportedly
favored by Li and a number of other officials. Keswick regarded
the scheme as a plausible one but thought that it would be very
damaging to the credit of the Chinese government in the money
markets of the world if it succeeded. Matheson and Company
agreed.[52]

Wu Ta-ch'eng replaced Li Ho-nien as director-general
of the Yellow River Works early in September 1888 because
the latter had failed to repair the breach. Cousins protested
to Li Hung-chang, reminding him of his promise to send for
Jardine's if the official supervisors failed, but Li maintained
that the appointment of Wu was an administrative change uncon-
nected with the progress of the work.[53] Morrison was then sent
to meet Wu at Chengchow, Honan, the site of the breach, to explain his plan, which proposed repairs with cement and a new
series of small dams.[54]

Morrison was courteously, though briefly, heard; he was
promised that the director would communicate with the firm if
necessary. Cousins also took Morrison to Tientsin: "The
Viceroy's manner being cordial and his assurances as vague
as before." Although rumors abounded that Wu Ta-ch'eng could
not close the breach, within the following months the breach
was closed with large quantities of cement, some of which had
been ordered through Jardine's by Detring. Morrison's regulating plan was filed for future reference. The bureaucracy
had proved again that its administrative resources were not
exhausted.

Chapter VI

THE IMPERIAL HOUSEHOLD

The most significant of Alexander Michie's activities
was his attempt, renewed over the course of several years,
to gain a favored place for Jardine, Matheson and Company at
the imperial court. William Keswick thought that the firm
should cultivate powerful provincial officials such as Li Hung-
chang, Liu Ming-ch'uan, and Chang Chih-tung.[1] Yet he and others
also thought that the final source of power might still be
found within the imperial court. The means by which Michie
expected to secure influence there were loans to the various
departments of the Imperial Household, the Nei-wu-fu, which
was concerned with the routine needs of daily life in the court,
the arrangement of festivals and minor secretarial duties.[2]

The Tung Yuen Bank, Michie's "style" with Nei-wu-fu
officials, had been established in 1870 to lend relatively
small sums on a systematic basis throughout the Chinese business
and political communities after the Ewo Bank had been closed.[3]
Negotiations preceding the 1884 loan had first brought Michie
and the Tung Yuen into contact with Peking officials and had
raised the possibility of further loan business on behalf of
the court.[4] Chen, Michie's Peking interpreter, had established
good relations with minor officials of the household at that
time. However, Michie and Chen learned quickly that the needs
of the household were unpredictable, depending upon the whims
of the imperial family, and among many officials they found a
strong reluctance to accept Tung Yuen loans. Occasionally
Michie would negotiate a loan, forward the Nei-wu-fu bond to

Shanghai and be in the process of transferring money when,
without warning, the official concerned would repudiate the
whole business, request immediate return of the bond and begin
repayment.[5] This was particularly embarrassing because of the
financial sacrifice made to provide this money when rates were
high in Shanghai.

Offers of competitive rates also made Michie's work
in Peking very difficult and large public loans nearly destroyed
it. The Hong Kong and Shanghai Bank's announcement of a loan of
Tls. 3,000,000 to the Chinese government, at 8 per cent per
annum, late in the summer of 1886 contrasted with Michie's
previous offer to the Nei-wu-fu of a consolidated loan at 12 per
cent per annum. Its manager again explained that the bank had
no idea it was interfering with Nei-wu-fu business; they had
assumed that the loan was needed for the navy program and
expected strong competition from the German Syndicate only.
Keswick attributed the misunderstanding to the intrigues of
Sheng Hsuan-huai while Michie insisted that the bank's action
had dealt a deliberate, "very nearly mortal blow" to Jardine's
influence in North China and that its innocence "would bring
a smile to Lufengluh's [Lo Feng-lu, secretary to Li Hung-chang]
big mouth."[7]

In order to preserve their connection with the Nei-wu-fu
Michie then proposed dealing with the separate departments of
the household rather than with the "high ministers" themselves,
accepting as security the departmental seals rather than what
he called "The General Seal of the Board." He believed that
having obtained the General Seal once, the firm had mistakenly
made it a sine qua non, forgetting that the use of this seal
involved publicity in Peking and exposed Ministers to the attacks
of censors who disapproved of foreign influence at the court,

or of specific terms offered. Departmental seals about whose
security Michie had no doubt, would, he argued, guarantee
anonymity and open many government doors hitherto closed.
After consulting Spence, who had some knowledge of the worth
of government seals, Keswick approved acceptance of departmental
seals for small loans but insisted that the Great Seal of the
Imperial Household be obtained for important amounts.[8]

Within the month Michie made six small loans to the
various departments and underscored the value of the connections
provided: "Apart from financial business I consider it important
to keep up a position in Peking as it is most convenient to have
the ear of the Manchus in a private way." He pointed out, as an
example, that private remonstrances at Peking "causing confidential
communications to pass from the Seventh Prince to the Viceroy"
had been the true cause of the French Syndicate's collapse at
Port Arthur.[9]

The value of a position at Peking had been reinforced
by the establishment of branches in the capital by both the
Hong Kong and Shanghai Bank and the Comptoir d'Escompte during
1885-1886, although the "foreign trade" conducted at the capital
was negligible. To compete with them, Michie occasionally dis-
regarded Shanghai's urgent call for funds.[10] Keswick, however,
objected to the retaining of funds without certain gain. When
the Nei-wu-fu requested, within one week, 280,000, 70,000 and
400,000 taels, Michie chided Shanghai for having been too anxious
about remittance and therefore allowing the bank to do the
business.[11]

Shortly after, he arranged a loan of Tls. 500,000 at
10 per cent per annum: "The struggle has been severe and has
probably not ended yet, and we have to come down to the time-
honored system of paying commissions to the officials." The

struggle, apparently, was against the blandishments of the bank
whose Peking branch had begun to solicit the custom of the court.
Michie was more confident than at any time since the Tung Yuen
opened: "I think we are at last getting over our troubles
in Peking and in a fair way towards a steady and profitable
business with the Palace, and in the way for any good things
that may turn up."[12] Security for the Tls. 500,000 consisted
of the seal of the treasury department of the Imperial Household
with "the signature of half a dozen great Ministers." Though
this was not the Great Seal of the Nei-wu-fu, only the seal
of its treasury, Michie claimed equal power for it because the
different departments of the Board "had been imperially appointed
with seals just as impossible to repudiate" for fear of jeopardiz-
ing imperial prestige.[13]

Michie further answered Keswick's doubts by explaining
that the revenues were in the control of the separate departments
and the heads of those departments were required to meet their
own engagements without reference to others. Therefore, department seals were good enough for moderate loans though he agreed
that a large loan demanded new terms and the Great Seal in order
to "put us in the front rank for any loan business."[14]

To further quiet doubts about the departmental security,
Michie revealed that most of the money borrowed by Chen to
fill the gap until sycee had arrived from Shanghai or Tientsin
for their Tls. 500,000 loan had been borrowed from officials
of the Board of Revenue and of the Nei-wu-fu itself, all of
whom charged current interest but none of whom questioned the
soundness of dealing with separate and financially autonomous
departments.[15]

After the bonds of the Imperial Household's treasury
department had been sent to Tientsin and secured in the firm's

safe, Michie congratulated Keswick on having established
Jardine's as "the confidential financier of the Empress,"
and on being head of a private firm which had lent the
largest sum ever borrowed by a department of the imperial
court. Keswick commented: "I am aware of the importance of
strengthening our hold upon the Nei-wu-fu in view of the
financial facilities required when the Emperor assumes the
reins of Government," but again insisted that further large
loans carry the Great Seal.[16]

In the autumn of 1886 the tempo of business accelerated.
Keswick wrote: "Mr Chen seems to have got in with the Nei-wu-fu
officials....Tls. 200,000 is required immediately for a festival."
This amount was provided at Tientsin by the Hong Kong and
Shanghai Bank because the firm had no available funds at
Shanghai or Tientsin. Chen had further success for several
months, as acting under Michie's instructions, he saw a number
of people "to whom a European would not have access" and
received promises of development contracts, including a very
large loan for railway construction, in exchange for small
loans to the bureaucracy.

Keswick, however, soon began once more to chafe about
the risk and the loss: "I am anxious to know from Michie whether
all these advances are leading on and if he looks for some big
loan being possible...in all this business there must be no
risk!" Michie replied optimistically: "Our position much
improved with the Minister of yamen or Boards, future prospects
good," though he admitted early in 1887 that he was disappointed
with the results of relations with the department and was hoping
for an important change of attitude later.[17]

His efforts to build the firm's position as "private
bankers to the Empress" and to influence decisions in Peking

reached a climax in 1888 when a series of small loans on the
security of the "lesser seals" was arranged in order to please
household officials. He had advised minimum pressure for quick
repayment of the loans totaling Tls. 900,000 in June 1888,
and argued that the amount involved was very little when compared to ultimate benefits should the firm maintain close
bonds with the court.[18] This argument rested on a conviction
that conservative antiforeign opinion among central officials
was steadily waning before the obvious fact of China's weakness
relative to the West and it assumed that progressive officials
would soon begin a Japanese type of development.

Keswick accepted Michie's reasoning, particularly when
signs seemed to indicate that the "great awakening" had truly
begun; Detring assured them that all of his almost visionary
development schemes had Li's full approval and would be carried
out with fullest foreign cooperation as soon as conservative
opposition in the Boards of Peking had been overcome.[19] But
as time passed without any sign of a thaw at the court or
any concrete gesture of favor toward the firm, Keswick began
again to write about his need for funds at Shanghai and urged
Michie to press the Nei-wu-fu for action or repayment. Persistent rumors about the unreliability of inferior seals and
the chaotic nature of Tung Yuen accounts also bothered him.
The bank had passed on to him a letter from a Manchu who
accused Chen of bungling by advancing to the Imperial Household on the security of the wrong seals. Keswick went through
the list of bonds himself and saw the documents "but as
they are in Chinese," he said "I was not much the wiser";
Mandl assured him that they were really promissory notes,
properly sealed. Nonetheless, Keswick urged Michie to "leave
no stone unturned to get our advances placed upon a regular

footing."[20] Michie replied that the nature of Nei-wu-fu
business, a network of personal contracts and personal
favoritism, precluded forcing it into the narrow paths of
business procedures in the West to which Keswick protested
that the firm had never intended to risk money in pursuit
of intangible benefits. Tls. 445,000 in payment was past due.
The departments of the household were to pay at once and those
bonds "lower than the Szu Yu Seal" were to be paid up in full
or renewed on higher seals at 12 per cent, or not less than
10 per cent per annum.[21]

Michie protested that these demands would be regarded
as peremptory by officials of the departments concerned and
would very likely blacken Jardine's reputation at the court.
Further correspondence, followed by an interview between
Michie and Keswick in Tientsin, resulted in Mandl's appointment as special assistant to Michie in Peking. Their first
joint task, in August, 1888, concerned the announced promotion
of En Yu, a palace official who had been a party to the granting
of Nei-wu-fu bonds and whose expected departure from Peking
appeared to be an excellent opportunity to pay up or to renew
under preferred seals without recourse to methods which Michie
deplored. Keswick warned that the firm was now prepared to
let prospective or collateral advantages, assumed on the basis
of official promises, pass by rather than risk very important
sums of money.[22]

Michie, apparently angered by the reiteration of the
"accountant's view," told En Yu and other officials that
Jardine, Matheson and Company had threatened repudiation of
their unconditional promissory notes unless one of their
alternatives for reorganizing the loans was accepted. Mandl
described official reaction as "offended and deeply suspicious

of our intentions."[23] Within a week Michie was dismissed
and replaced by Donald Spence, who hastened from Tientsin
under instructions to correct "the hopeless condition of
drift into which Michie had allowed things to lapse."

Spence's first act was to change the Chinese name of
the firm in Peking from Tung Yuen to its usual treaty port
style, Ewo, after learning from Chen's replacement that Tung
Yuen was regarded with distrust "at the Treasury (Hupu)
and among the offices of the Imperial Household."[24] Spence
set himself to repair the damage, first by assuring officials
that the promissory notes had not been repudiated and then by
assuring them that Ewo stood ready to meet their present and
future needs. He reported that Michie and Chen had been working
through "inferior channels," i.e. the departments, instead
of contacting the high officials of the household "through
whom I am negotiating a general settlement which promises
further Palace and Board of Revenue business."[25] Tseng Chi-
tse told Spence that the government recognized the validity
of Jardine's claims upon the Imperial Household and a Nei-wu-fu
official promised that some loans would be repaid, others
renewed, and perhaps others negotiated on a new basis. Keswick
sent dispatches to Fu Ching-tang, head of the household, pointedly
mentioning that the daily wants of the emperor's table had been
met by Tung Yuen in order to accommodate the Nei-wu-fu and re-
commending that they, in return, be willing to reorganize their
debts. These blunt demands had been suggested by Tseng Chi-tse
who, apparently, did not agree with Michie's filial ideas.[26]

In May, 1889, the Hong Kong Bank lent Tls. 500,000 to
the Nei-wu-fu, Tls. 400,000 of which was paid to Matheson and
Company within two days.[27] Shortly after, Spence began a series
of meetings with Fu Ching-tang which finally resulted in the
consolidation of unpaid loans and the granting of two new loans.[28]

They also discussed larger loans which Fu had been empowered
to negotiate on behalf of the Board of Revenue; Keswick wel-
comed the definite establishment of a center of loan activity
rivaling Li's yamen.[29]

These Nei-wu-fu loans were to be repaid in fifteen
annual installments, through June, 1892, by the Hoppo of
Canton acting under imperial command. Nei-wu-fu weights, sealed
with the seal of Fu Ching-tang were sent to Shanghai, then
forwarded by steamer to Canton "with instructions that the
Seals are not to be broken until the Paid Installment of loans
A and B fall due."[30]

Once the Michie loans had been placed on this firmer
basis, relations with Nei-wu-fu officials became more cautious,
particularly since evidence of the household's power to create
policy remained slight. In his congratulations to Spence, John
McGregor, the new head of the firm, referred to troubles the
firm had had with palace loans:

> The Palace officials are a hard lot. In clean borrowing
> China must learn to act like more civilized countries. The
> eagerness of foreigners to sue for her favours in the last
> few years or so has given some of her officials false
> notions of what is properly possible...one can now see how
> the Shanghai bankers were bullied and their advances finally
> repudiated by the Palace. I suppose the legation people con-
> sider that you have obtained a triumph in compelling the
> attendance of the Nei-wu-fu people at your own house?[31]

Yet, through 1889 and the early nineties close relations
were maintained with the Nei-wu-fu as a possible key to large
business because of its connection with the Hupu. The firm
informed officials of both that it was interested in loans
which carried the security of an imperial edict, would lend

brokers an aura of official prestige, and put an unimpeach-
able lien on customs revenue. Specifically, the firm
wanted issuance of any all-purpose loan which might be needed
for railways and large engineering projects because loans
were still seen as a means of influencing the decisions of
the Chinese-Manchu oligarchy.

Building upon Michie's achievements (and his mistakes)
Spence had gained the confidence of Hsiang Ming, of the
Nei-wu-fu, and Fu Ching-tang through whom he secured information which, though often inaccurate, several times allowed
the firm to consult London in advance about a possible loan
or contract. They also helped to fill in what had been an
extremely vague picture of relations among officials at
Peking. Fu confirmed Keswick's guess that Tseng Chi-tse was
not in a position to initiate policy. Tseng's reputation
as a Westernizer had aroused the hostility of conservative
officials and neutralized his advice. Prince Ch'un was described as possessing decisive power and Fu assured Spence
that a number of Peking officials, including "progressives,"
opposed Li Hung-chang and his followers regardless of the
merits of any plan Li presented. There was obviously strong
factional conflict within the bureaucracy.[32]

Such confidences hardened Keswick's resolve to press
the firm's plans at both Tientsin and Peking until such
time as one or the other faction became obviously dominant
within the bureaucracy: "We must keep in touch with all
influential parties, try not to offend any of them and
if a request must be refused let it be done with reasons
given and every courtesy."[33]

However, even Peking sources were unable or unwilling
to furnish specific details of the government's financial
state. The bank believed that both central and provincial

treasuries were nearly empty from the time of the war with
France, that all signs indicated expenditure greatly in
excess of revenue, and that another round of large loans
to meet current deficits and to further "progressive" works
could be expected.[34] In this situation Keswick thought his
firm was the perfect broker because of its solid reputation
in China and its ability to enlist the support of London's
largest finance houses and banks.

However, overconfidence had led the firm to alert
Matheson and Company several times about loans which were
not, in the end, requested by the Chinese government. By
the late eighties, these false starts and experience with
the Nei-wu-fu made the firm less sure of the value of loans
made to influence future business. Each transaction with
the China bureaucracy was considered entirely upon its own
merits and no loans were made to provincial officials on
the security of the provincial seal. The governor of
Shantung, "Ching-Yew" (Chang Yao), met a courteous refusal
when he applied for Tls. 500,000 at 7 per cent, offering
his seal as security. This policy coincided with Robert
Hart's policy of centralizing financial power at Peking and
restoring central authority as a first step to reform, in
order to enhance China's attraction for Western capital.[35]

This new policy had come indirectly out of Nei-wu-fu
business and directly out of negotiations with the Hupu
over Tls. 4,000,000 which Mandl believed was to be used for
further Yellow River repairs and general military purposes.
At first report the Shanghai office had decided not to telegraph Matheson and Company since neither agent knew whether
the loan would be in silver or gold "but in either case interest
must be payable to us in China and, in the case of gold,
at telegraphic transfer rate of the day every six months

or preferably every three."[36]

The bank's assurance that the Hupu's query was serious, followed by communication with Matheson and Company, brought a statement of terms; 8 per cent for a silver loan extending over a period of years, repayment commencing before ten years. Payment and repayment in Peking were to be avoided because of the probable loss on exchange when profit margins were narrow: "The expense incident to floating a loan on the London market and agency for repayment are heavier than is usually imagined." Sterling bonds would be issued in London bearing the official seal and the signature of the Chinese Minister for the equivalent of the amount in silver which the Chinese government asked to borrow: "Jardine Matheson would give the Chinese government their guarantee to be responsible to them for any loss consequent upon fluctuations in Exchange. Silver per se will not be looked at by the financiers and we have to make special arrangements to undertake the liability."[37]

Michie, while still representative in Peking, had warned that demands for an imperial edict guaranteeing loans could be construed as an attempt to slight the dignity of the Chinese government and he had suggested that the Seal of the Hupu, communicated by the Tsungli Yamen to the British Minister, would be sufficient security.[38] Keswick did not object to the Seal of the Hupu but since imperial edicts had appeared in the Peking Gazette authorizing the loans made by the Hong Kong Bank he did not see how subsequent edicts involved any principle. In the case of the Tls. 4,000,000 loan, Spence believed that an imperial edict would certainly be given before either the Hupu or the Board of Admiralty, parties to the loan, would use their official seals for such a large amount.[39]

Speculation ended when Fu Ching-tang informed Spence that the loan would not be wanted after all; for some months after the firm's alleged mishandling of the Nei-wu-fu every proposal to the Chinese government met with coolness. In their dealings with the Nei-wu-fu, and the Hupu, Jardine, Matheson and Company learned something of the intentions and limitations of the central government. They also learned that specific development proposals to willing provincial authorities deserved more attention than the pursuit of influence within central government departments. The firm began to focus upon the financing and building of railways.

Chapter VII

RAILWAYS AND LOANS

Railways had always been regarded by Jardine's as
the key to essential and widespread change in the Chinese
economy. Loans and other financial services, believed to be
a prior condition of railway contracts, were offered because
the firm thought that once a railway system had linked China's
interior with Shanghai, Canton, and Tientsin, an enormous
development of industry and of domestic and foreign trade
would follow.

Railway schemes had been discussed among Western
merchants in China since the 1840's when a group of merchants
had considered the suggestion of a railway from Calcutta to
Canton,[1] and the following years saw the drawing of many
general plans of railway routes to be constructed "when
China enters the civilized world."[2] Rebellion, the opium
trade, and effective Western exclusion from the interior
delayed more concrete plans until the sixties, when a
Jardine partner (M.A. MacLeod) inspired MacDonald Stephenson
to draw up a comprehensive railway scheme for China similar
to that which he had sponsored in India.[3] Chinese officials
were not receptive. In rejecting the proposal Li Hung-chang
stated: "railroads would only be beneficial to China if
undertaken by the Chinese themselves and constructed under
their own management."[4]

However, Jardine's persisted and began to organize
a company to build a line from Shanghai to Woosung, connecting
the great trade center with its outer port twelve miles

eastward. Shanghai was also chosen because the firm believed in demonstrating the value of an efficient railway to officials and merchants in the major treaty port. The "Woosung Road Company" was organized as a joint-stock enterprise in March 1865 (200 shares issued) with Jardine's as managing agents.[5] A number of foreign merchants backed the scheme and shares were also "widely distributed among the Chinese business community."[6] Without official permission (although there are indications that the taotai of Shanghai had been approached privately),[7] the company began through Chinese agents to buy land along the route, ostensibly for a horse road: costs were so far beyond original estimates that the scheme was temporarily abandoned in 1867 and the company liquidated.[8]

F.B. Johnson, acting in the hope that officials had become more receptive, revived the Shanghai-Woosung plans in 1872 and began to prepare the ground over the next two years, ordering the Ransome and Rapier small engine and cars, acquiring land, again for a "road," appointing Morrison engineer, and in July, 1874, registering the company under limited liability with the head office given as Canton. A capital of Tls. 100,000 had been raised among the Shanghai community, foreign and Chinese,[9] and the opening of the first portion of the railway, as far as Kangwan, took place on June 30, 1876. During the same month, Sir Thomas Wade, British Minister, was making preparations to meet Li Hung-chang at Chefoo to settle British claims over the murder of August Margary in Yunnan.[10]

In July receipts averaged $40 to $60 daily and operations were "highly satisfactory" until on August 5, 1876, the Shanghai office announced the death of a Chinese on the line.[11] Details of the accident were obscure, but the company agreed to compensate the man's family while work on completion of the line went forward. Johnson did not belive the accident

had been arranged by local officials although a number of
official protests had followed.[12]

At Chefoo where Wade and Li had begun the talks which
resulted in the "Chefoo Convention,"[13] one of the firm's agents
reported to Shanghai that Li proposed that the Chinese government purchase the line because it had been unauthorized and
"he thought railways should be in Government control."[14] Wade
advised Jardine's privately that it would be best to agree
to sell since the railway had been built without official
approval and could not be defended by the British government.[15]
Jardine's assented, provided that Wade would obtain no less
than Tls. 300,000 for the entire plant.[16] Johnson thought the
firm would very likely profit from a sale to the Chinese government because he assumed that Li's desire to control and operate
the railway indicated that a Chinese railroad company, similar
to the China Merchants Steam Navigation Company, was about
to be organized.[17] Since the Woosung Road Company included
Chinese shareholders, and was meant as a demonstration to
impress and convince Chinese officials, the intention was to
create interests which, they hoped, would lead to an alteration
of the treaty or at least to a mitigation of official resistance
to railways. The prospect of sale to the Chinese government
left the firm unconcerned about the future operation of the
line.[18] The railway had demonstrated the firm's fitness
for such work to Li Hung-chang, with whom decisions on the
inevitable industrialization program must lie.

Morrison was instructed to get an interview with
Li through Tong King-sing, if opportunity presented itself,
and to assure him of the willingness and ability of the
firm to float loans, construct railways, open mines, or do
anything that required influence or capital to back it.[19]

Morrison's instructions summarize the firm's long-term aim, to be suppliers of equipment and capital for the projects initiated by the high Chinese bureaucracy. The Shanghai-Woosung Railway was, for its managers, a pawn sacrificed in the interest of those greater ends. Negotiations showed the firm's willingness to work closely with Chinese officials while surrendering control of the line as a generous sign of goodwill. When the negotations were transferred to Hu Kuang-yung (Wu Si-nan) silk merchant, banker, and intermediary between the government and foreign merchants,[20] Jardine's had amicable dealings with him. On November 25, 1876, "after much discussion, which has lasted for hours, the Railway has been sold to the Chinese government for Tls. 285,000 Shanghai sycee, as this will leave £10,000 for commissions and interest we cannot well complain."[21]

Morrison, accompanied by other Jardine, Matheson and Company staff had seen Li in the first week of September when Li again declared himself strongly in favor of railways, repeating, however, his 1863 remarks about the importance of Chinese control with approved foreign assistance in planning and construction.[22] He told Morrison (perhaps ironically), that he quite recognized the importance of the Shanghai-Woosung line.[23] He repeated that Jardine's would have a good chance of receiving agency business in connection with railways and mining enterprise since the firm's position as "bankers and financial agents" was excellent.[24]

Further examples of the firm's persistence in pursuit of railway loans and contracts through Li came in the late eighties just after Li presented a memorial to the throne advocating a Kaiping railway extension which would link Tientsin and the coast.[25] The memorial stressed military

advantages over economic, but referred to both, in making a
request "for the experimental introduction of a railway at
Tientsin and other places in order to facilitate the movement
of troops and the transport of materials of war and to increase
the profits of the mercantile classes."[26]

Imperial permission followed and the Kaiping Railway
Company became the China Railway Company; a prospectus was
distributed on April 12, 1887. Ten thousand shares were to
be issued at Tls. 100 per share. The company's difficulty in
enlisting domestic capital, though the Hong Kong Shanghai Bank
acted as its agent, has been explained by Kent: "The idea
of joint-stock enterprise, unless under foreign supervision
fails to appeal to the generality of Chinese investors."[27]
It was exactly this element of foreign control, so attractive
to investors, which Li Hung-chang and all other modernizing
officials were determined to exclude from railway development
and other "modern" projects. These projects were meant to
support China's independence, not to compromise with the
presence of treaty-protected foreign interests; foreign
syndicate railway schemes were therefore refused.[28] The firm
did not regard itself as part of any syndicate. When the new
company was announced, Jardine's agents immediately offered
their services to Li and to officials in Peking known to be
close to Prince Ch'un, who was credited with promoting a comprehensive scheme which would make the Kaiping line the beginning of a great trunk system requiring an initial investment of Tls. 14,000,000. Michie admitted that rumors of the
prince's scheme might be unfounded but, if true, meant the
start of an era with limitless prestige for the company
financing and controlling such a program.[29]

The sense that events seemed to be moving toward some
new solution of China's problems in the spring and summer of

1887 has been described. When J. Keswick visited Tientsin he
had several interviews with Detring, "Chang," head of the
Ordnance Department and a nephew of Li Hung-chang, the
Tientsin Haikwan Taotai, Ch'eng-fu, in charge of Port Arthur
works, and Li Hung-chang himself; as a result, Keswick's
reports to Hong Kong became as optimistic as Michie's had often
been. In one of them he said: "We seem to be at a deadlock
as regards railroads and loans and we must await events to get
us out of it but I am sure we are on the eve of great activity
in the construction of public works in China."[30]

Li Hung-chang offered the firm contracts for heavy cannons
and building materials required in the fortification of Wei-hai-wei,
explaining that he wished to compensate for their disappointment
over Port Arthur contracts, and he expressed appreciation of
the firm's desire to assist his program, at which Keswick exulted:
"We appear to be the only people at present capable of putting
through any business of consequence. The French and German
Syndicates are paralyzed and the energy of private firms, although
unabated, does not seem to avail them much against our superior
ability and zeal."[31]

Li's assurances of friendship were so convincing that
Keswick assented without hesitation to his suggestion that
the firm help construct the Taku-Tientsin Railroad by lending
Tls. 150,000 at below current interest, i.e. 5 1/2 per cent.
A contract was signed within the week (July 1887). Keswick
explained to London: "The profit will only be what we can make
in Exchange but the business is very valuable in other ways."
He added that this loan, coming on the heels of their railroad
victory in Formosa, was sure to establish Jardine's place in
the imminent China railroad boom.[32]

However, through that summer the American Syndicate
(whose prime component was Russell and Company) had been rumored

to be offering comprehensive railway schemes and money at the
very low rate of 4 per cent and all other business took place
against this backdrop; Michie telegraphed (July 25, 1887) that
a loan of Tls. 2,500,000 had just been made "at about 4%, to
match the Americans" by the German Syndicate to the Imperial
Telegraph Administration "in return presumably, for placing
Mickiewicz's telephone along the Government lines."[33] The firm,
assuming that Ma Kie-tchong (Ma Chien-chung) and Sheng Hsuan-huai
had been bribed heavily, concluded that:

> This loan with its conditions attached will not affect
> the rate for public loans generally or lead the Chinese
> to think they can get money on the basis of this new
> American Syndicate's rate of interest.[34]

By agreement with Matheson and Company, Jardine agents
had named 5 1/2 per cent per annum as the minimum price of any
money offered although always, of course, they were to try for
the highest rate they could get. Interest rates were never
so high in London as in Shanghai and Hong Kong and if a particular
transaction made it necessary, the firm was prepared to borrow
in London.[35]

One week later Michie telegraphed that the American
Syndicate seemed certain to secure a contract for the financing
and building of the long-awaited railroad network:

> The success with which the agents of the American
> Syndicate have carried through the preliminaries of their
> comprehensive, gigantic scheme is amazing and the history
> of the negotiations, if were known, will be interesting.[36]

Keswick assumed that "Black" Butler of Russell and Company had
induced Tseng Chi-tse to support their proposals in Peking by
arguing that Americans were less repugnant to the conservatives.[37]
Late in August it was announced that an agreement had been reached,

though a formal contract would not be signed for ninety days; the firm's agents were instructed to point out the dangers of the American plan to Li Hung-chang and to officials in Peking. "...the only way is to frighten the Chinese, already alarmed at their own rashness." Matheson and Company in the meantime would inquire about arranging a sterling loan of £1,000,000 if the Americans were repudiated and James Keswick wrote that "he would try to get some comprehensive proposal laid before the proper officials in Peking (but who are they?) to provide money, railways and everything connected with it."[38] He had written to Michie: "Are the Chinese Government really thinking about the construction of railways beyond the little line they are now building and its extension to Peking? If so we are drawing up proposals to include a Peking-Yangtze line."[39] Michie confessed that his sources in Peking could not say with certainty that the American contract would be signed or that railways had been authorized.

Morrison drew up new proposals which Michie and Mandl presented at Li's yamen and to "a number of people living in Peking," Tseng Chi-tse's support being especially solicited; yet it is an interesting comment on the difficulties of dealing with a divided and revenue-starved government that Michie, after five years, could not be sure that he was in touch with those responsible for final decisions. He could not even judge the strength of Tseng's influence. Morrison's critique of the American scheme was put into "good Chinese" and sent by Michie to the Fifth Prince (I-tsung) leader of the conservative faction, in the hope that this would arouse him to fight such "a mortgaging of revenue" in the highest councils.[40]

Sir John Walsham was shown Morrison's alternative plan, was "enthusiastic and interested" but gave no promise of any action. Mandl believed that the American scheme would not

succeed, in any case, because it was impossible to trust any
of the officials connected with it. He advised a policy of
"wait and see."[41]

Michie discussed Morrison's plan several times with
Tseng Chi-tse who thought the acceptance of any comprehensive
scheme most unlikely, that the American Syndicate plan would
not finally be approved and that railways would come to China
piece by piece, not as a full program. The firm was disappointed.
Michie wrote: "After all the great things the world expects
from the reputed author of the great awakening this hand-to-
mouth policy does not point to an early public loan of great
magnitude." Before the end of August the American offer had
been refused.[42]

The firm's interest in railways also led to experiment-
ing with marginal schemes because belief persisted in the value
of demonstration despite failure in 1877. In 1884, Gaston Galy,
representing the Deccanville Railway Company, French manufacturers of a small-gauge system, signed a ten-year contract
with Jardine's under which the firm pledged itself to act as
agent for the introduction of the Deccanville in China. Galy
was to act as their engineer and consultant, and his experimental line, engine, coaches, and rails had been sent out in
1884-1885, demonstrated at Hong Kong and Canton without success,
and finally sent to Tientsin in the hope that Li Hung-chang
would be attracted: "A couple of miles of line of 30 inches
gauge were laid in the plain at the back of British settlement."
In August 1886, Michie believed that the experiment had impressed Li's yamen so much that it would be advisable to order
enough Deccanville equipment for the first Kaiping extension:
"Order out a quantity of both the passenger line and the mud-
carrying line," he wrote "as the chances of disposing of them
are very good."[43] At Michie's direction Galy drew up a

comprehensive plan showing how the Deccanville system was
suitable for almost every possible railway need in China,
including a trans-Mongolian line across the Gobi to Urga
(Ulan Bator), though Keswick cautioned that Jardine, Matheson
and Company would not be interested in placing orders unless
sales were absolutely guaranteed.[44]

Contrary to Michie's expectations, Li Hung-chang placed
no order. Galy then went to Peking where permission to demonstrate
was refused for several months until officials suggested to
Michie that a gift of the Deccanville line to the Empress would
be the most effective kind of demonstration and would, undoubtedly,
lead to a greater understanding of the value of these machines.
Michie seized on the idea and strongly recommended that a gift
be made of the plant. Galy agreed, and both wrote to Shanghai,
provoking Keswick's irritated reply:

> A perusal of these facts gives me the impression that
> even if Mr. Galy succeeded in the course he was pursuing
> in Peking the only result would be permission to try to
> lay up an experimental line in the precincts of the Imperial
> Palace, or to Wu-Shi-Shan, at our expense, the only induce-
> ment offered being some problematical advantage by and by.[45]

Keswick demanded practical evidence that the imperial government was seriously interested in railroad development. The
failure of the Deccanville demonstration in Tientsin, under
the eyes of one of the few powerful officials interested in
railways, had made him much less sanguine than the perennially
confident Michie, whom he advised to get a definite offer or
to induce the palace to consider another sterling loan as a
gesture of intent before such a gift could be made.[46]

Michie saw Tseng Chi-tse who suggested that the plant
be sold to the court for a nominal sum, Tls. 4,000, because
its presence would help him to advance railroad development

in China. Keswick demurred again:

> Marquis Tseng I am sure means well and if he can would
> put business our way in return for the complacent surrender
> to him of a line of railraod costing nearly Tls. 25,000
> but...he would not have it in his power to place a large
> contract in our hands no matter how anxious he might be to do
> so.[47]

Galy insisted that a daily demonstration in the imperial court
would inevitably bring large orders for "its extensive employ-
ment throughout China," but Keswick argued that a sacrifice gift
would not lead to large railroad business or mollify those
conservative officials who were opposed to railways on grounds
of principle. However, he conceded that he would consider the
matter again if:

> The free presentation of the railroad could be made to
> tie in with something else--the concession for the construction
> of the Tientsin-Peking line?--a tangible quid-pro-quo, not
> a shadowy promise from the Marquis Tseng which with the
> highest and most honorable intentions the very nature of
> the business would prevent him carrying out.[48]

The bureaucracy remained unconvinced and the line unsold.

Morrison's elaborate memorial on railways, presented
to Tseng Chi-tse in the summer of 1887 on the advice of Sir John
Walsham, had outlined major trunk lines, an extension of the
Northern line, and estimated total costs with no result. In
June 1889, the firm's latest information was that Prince Ch'un
and Li Hung-chang were the men "with whom the ultimate decision
as to the construction of trunk lines and the methods of providing funds will rest;" the memorial was taken from the files,

its Chinese style checked and a new copy sent to Li Hung-chang.

Some months later Tong King-sing told Cousins that a
trunk line, Canton-Hankow, would be constructed in 1890 and that
a large loan would contribute to its preparation; Li Han-chang,
Li Hung-chang's brother, would supervise the Southern section
while the viceroy directed in the North and the line would be
built with foreign capital. Yet rumors also persisted that the
government had decided to postpone the building of any major
railway line for five years and that the conservatives were
in full control of the court, castigating both Liu Ming-ch'uan
and Li Hung-chang for what had already been accomplished. Old
arguments about the destruction of the people's livelihood were
reinforced by depicting the military threat which foreign-built
lines might pose to the capital itself and a long-term scheme
proposed by Chang Chih-tung on the basis of foreign exclusion
and Chinese self-sufficiency seemed likely to block all railway
building for some years.[49]

Many in the firm agreed that Chang Chih-tung's Yangtze
trunk scheme, if accepted, would certainly mean an indefinite
postponement of foreign-directed railroad building. However,
this did not diminish their activity. Robert Inglis of the
Shanghai staff was sent to Peking in October 1889 to conduct loan
negotiations and attempt integration of these negotiations with
railway contracts: "The reason for Inglis' stay in Peking is
very well understood by those interested in Chinese finance,"
Keswick wrote. The greater part of his correspondence with
Shanghai in 1890 and 1891 centered upon a loan of Tls. 30,000,000
sought by the Board of Revenue for general purposes.[50] Details
of an offer to lend this amount, made by an American-German
syndicate were first telegraphed to Shanghai in May 1890; they
included the repayment of interest and capital in silver at

4 1/2 per cent interest and 2 1/2 per cent commission for floating.
Macgregor refused to believe that any syndicate would, at that
time, exchange in silver at 4 1/2 per cent without a great number
of collateral guarantees or advantages, none of which were specified
in Inglis' copy of the Hupu's memo.[51] In order to test the complex rumors and determine the content of various offers, the firm
resorted to what had become normal practice: "Let him (a Mr.
Liu) be very active and close in his inquiries and keep you fully
posted on what goes on--for the douceurs he dispenses he ought
to have access to all letters or Memorials upon this and other
subjects." Macgregor complimented his efforts: "I note with
much satisfaction the connection for information as to what is
being done in high quarters which you have been able to establish
and trust that something tangible will come of this long period
of waiting and negotiation."[52]

Another important means of forming judgments in these
matters was "intelligent surmise" regarding the relative
importance of any high official, especially Li Hung-chang's weight
in Peking which Inglis was asked to measure several times in the
early nineties. Cousins and Mandl frequently commented on the
same subject from Tientsin.[53]

In June 1890, three separate loans were being discussed.
The thirty-million-tael loan, then believed to be in Li Hung-
chang's disposition and intended largely for railways, a five to
seven-million-tael admiralty loan and another Hupu loan of
uncertain amount. Macgregor had proposed to Hong Kong and Shanghai
Bank that the bank and his firm "maintain a friendly marginal
competition" whereby the Peking sphere of action would be left
to Jardine's and Tientsin to the bank, each promising to help
the other. If any of the loans were found to be in the gift
of either Li Hung-chang or central officials exclusively, the

arrangement would call for a two-thirds settlement of the loan
at the place negotiated and one-third at the other. This allowed
the bank and Jardine's to concentrate either upon Li's yamen or
the various Peking boards without injuring each other. The bank
agreed to informal cooperation.[54]

In Peking Inglis had daily interviews with Hupu officials,
Fu Ching-tang, and officials of the admiralty from whom he learned
that the five to seven-million-tael loan would be merged into the
large loan, naval requirements being met by the Hupu.

In July 1890, Inglis was told that the Chinese government
would not borrow Tls. 30,000,000 for railways on a gold basis,
thus checking the firm's plans since Matheson and Company had just
informed its China representative that they would not support an
offer in silver. Russell and Company, the Deutsche-Asiatische
Bank and a French group were prepared to offer proposals for a
silver loan and a "phenomenal" offer of a silver loan had been
made by an Austrian financier at 4 1/2 per cent with 2 1/2 per
cent commission, equaling the initial terms offered by the American-
German Syndicate.[55] Inglis further learned that the whole loan
had become a duel between high authorities in Peking and Li
Hung-chang whose brother, Li Han-chang, was accepting offers in
Peking which rivaled those being made to the Hupu. (Li Han-chang
described himself as the director-general of a planned National
Railway Company.)[56] Departing from their agreement with the
bank, the firm sent Li Han-chang a secret proposal offering
Tls. 30,000,000 on a gold basis, at 6 1/2 per cent, repayment
to be over fifty years; Li Han-chang rejected their terms within
a week, stating that he had been offered "any amount of money at
4 1/2 per annum on a gold basis."[57]

Through the autumn of 1890 Inglis' reports read as a series
of encouraging signs followed by dashed hopes. A Mr. Wang, who had
described himself as intimate with officials of the Hupu, produced

no results after six weeks of promises and delays. Yet Inglis insisted that "we are gradually approaching touch with the persons most influential in controlling the disposition of the Loan if and when it is to be actually settled." Meanwhile, he had made two small loans to Fu Ching-tang who had told him that the palace was in urgent need of funds and therefore likely to approve the big loan. Fu warned, however, that officials of the Hupu were wary of Jardine, Matheson and Company and still maintained that the Chinese government had paid more than was necessary on exchange for the Shen Chi Ying loan of 1884. Inglis rebutted by reference to the subsequent change in the relative value of gold and silver as evidence of official misjudgment of the charges on the loan.[58]

The matter was stalemated until early in the new year when Prince Ch'un died. He had been head of the Shen Chi Ying at the time of the 1884 loan, had often encouraged arms contracts negotiated by Jardine's and at the time of his death was supposed to have been one of those deciding on the large loan. Inglis was ready without delay to become acquainted with "the people of the Yamen or those few high officials who are at all likely to occupy the position left vacant so that when a successor is named you may lose no time in handing him a letter with the Ewo offer for the thirty million loan."[59] It was soon clear that I-K'uang, Prince Ch'ing, who had been one of the two controllers of the Admiralty Board since 1885, would have the power to allocate the loan; therefore, Inglis made arrangements to obtain copies of his letters, to note his visitors, and to gauge his attitude toward loans and railways.[60]

Macgregor assured Inglis that the firm was quite prepared to offer for and negotiate both the "Big Loan and the Hupu Loan," terms for the latter being Tls. 5,000,000 at 6 1/2 per cent per annum on a fifty-year basis (with no repayment of

principal), interest payable in sterling and imperial edict
demanded. These terms were unattractive to the Hupu officials
yet Inglis persisted for several months in Peking and was so
confident of the firm's ultimate success that he refused to
promise anything to "a group of Censors who offered to memorialize
the Throne on our behalf."[61] Macgregor, however, suggested that
"presents be sent on the occasion of the forthcoming festival"
to H.E. Hsiang Ming and Censor Tsai, both of whom claimed to
influence the placing of the big loan. Tsai soon informed Inglis
that 10 per cent commission would be required by those granting
the loan; Macgregor wired that Tls. 3,000,000 commission was
"simply an attempt at an exorbitant squeeze." The firm authorized
Inglis to promise a "cumshaw" of 3 per cent, or Tls. 900,000,
or less if possible, and advised him when dealing about the big
loan to make capital out of the failure in July 1891 of Russell
and Company, recent competitors in loan business (who had over-
speculated in sugar). He was to imply that the choice of brokers
was narrower than the Chinese seemed to believe.[62] In October
1891, Inglis learned that the big loan would not be considered
by the admiralty or the Hupu that year; he was instructed "to
keep in touch with H.E. Hsiang Ming and other officials likely
to influence the business" in order to raise the matter in the
new year.[63]

But the first months of 1892 were poor months in the
China trade. Russell and Company's failure was followed by the
collapse of the "New Oriental Bank" and the bankruptcy of the
Hong Kong and Shanghai Bank's Shanghai compradore, a man of
great influence in the treaty port communities. William Keswick,
writing to G.L. Montgomery, Jardine's New York agents, spoke of
"how disastrous Eastern trade has been for some time," and a
confidential statement of the firm's assets circulated among their
agents to allay suspicion of Jardine, Matheson and Company's

strength. It stated that $8,600,000 (US) was represented as capital in the firm's 1891 balance sheet, $7,500,000 of which was almost immediately liquid: "A very ample amount which provides the utmost security for all contingencies." Keswick also assured New York that the rating accorded the firm by the Association of New York Bankers was in no danger of declining since the firm's working capital (more than $1,000,000 in gold, absolutely intact) was very considerably in excess of the sum required.[64] All these assurances concerned the China House and did not mention Matheson and Company's considerable resources, presumably at their disposal. Nevertheless, the financial panic soured enthusiasm for high finance in China; Peking and Tientsin negotiations were ordered suspended, and intense interest in loans did not revive until just before the Sino-Japanese War.

Opposition between China's loose administrative structure, that weak central control which allowed Li Hung-chang to act virtually as Foreign Minister from his provincial base, and the extraneous forces discouraging too much provincial autonomy, especially the Inspector-General of Customs, reached a climax in the months of transition just before and after the Treaty of Shimonoseki. The swift intensification of national rivalries affected every aspect of Western presence in China, presaging the later emergence from this internal tension of two policies among the Great Powers--that favoring spheres of exclusive influence based upon provincial autonomy and that favoring the Open Door maintained by a mildly reformed central authority, financially and diplomatically supported by interested powers.[65] The firm had dealt with both central and provincial officials for many years, maintaining a foothold at each administrative

level in order to cooperate in all progressive initiatives.
They were aware of Hart's belief that a strong central authority,
firmly controlling revenues and their disposition, would be an
essential prerequisite of wider reforms but could see no way in
which a private firm might act upon this belief.[66] Their abortive
cooperation with other large Western firms might have increased
their political as well as their commercial weight, but none of
these had been really successful; the firm accepted the bureaucracy as it was without any conscious pressure upon the balance
between Peking and the provinces.

In the first six months of 1894, as tensions increased
between China and Japan over Korea, Li Hung-chang again sought
money and arms.[67] At Jardine offices there were many rumors
about large loans: "Li Hung-chang is reported desirous of raising
a loan of Tls. 1,000,000 on the China Merchants' steamers,"[68] and
Matheson and Company telegraphed that they could float such a
loan at 95 and 5 per cent providing as usual that an imperial
edict were issued as guarantee.[69] Also they again stressed
cooperation with the Hong Kong and Shanghai Bank.[70]

Sheng Hsuan-huai[71] and Lo Feng-lu accepted Jardine's
terms for Krupp and Armstrong armaments which Li might require
on short notice and Keswick secured interviews with high officials
of the admiralty in Peking to propose that the firm lend £1,500,000,
an amount which Nei-wu-fu officials said was urgently needed for
"improvements." But Keswick found that "their ideas of the rate
of interest makes a Sterling loan quite out of the question"
particularly since "the German element" in Tientsin had offered
to put through a sterling loan against a shipment of arms.[72]

Mr. Bevis (who had replaced Cameron in 1889 at the bank)
informed Keswick while he was in Peking that the bank had arranged
to meet the admiralty's request on a silver basis, the whole matter
having been negotiated through Sir Robert Hart who "wished to

centralize as much as possible" all future China loans in order
to diminish the powers and interests of the various viceroys,
governors and taotais as a first step to administrative reform.[73] Keswick approved both of the loan and the idea behind
it, since there was no chance for floating even a sterling loan
in London that autumn and the firm had no prejudice against dealing
directly with Peking if possible.

After China's military collapse and administrative in-
competence had been demonstrated to the world, a few weeks
before the signing of the treaty of Shimonoseki, Jardine's had
been urged by the British Minister in China to prepare for
the coming great contest between German and British interests
in "this stricken country." He predicted that German commercial
and financial groups would exploit China's "disintegration"
through offers of financial assistance, offers which had to be
countered if Britain was to hold and expand her commercial lead
in the Far East.[74] There was a great deal of correspondence
in this vein during the final months of the war, speculating as
to its possible outcome or its effect upon trade, but there was
no evident change in the firm's willingness to continue cooperation on its own account with the officials whose limited policies
had brought the country to its spectacular defeat.

Chinese forces had lost every battle. Wooden cannon
balls painted to resemble real equipment symbolized the mis-
appropriation of funds and the administrative corruption which
had characterized self-strengthening development under official
control. Some partners of the firm still assumed, however,
that the modernizing faction in the bureaucracy would
emerge unscathed from the treaty negotiations and would become,
at last, effective agents of a Japan-like regeneration which
would forestall the collapse expected by so many observers.
Apparently they did not think that the shock of defeat would

necessarily bring changed attitudes within the entire bureaucracy entailing a great wave of progressive Westernization;
rather their attitude was determinedly pragmatic, geared to
immediate events and to continuation of business on behalf of
those officials with whom they had dealt prior to the full
exposure of China's weaknesses.

The firm had evidence that some officials were working
for a renewed China even in the hour of defeat. Before an
armistice had been declared, while the British government and
others were exploring the possibility of mediation, Chang Chih-
tung had wired to ask if the firm would consider a gold loan
for £1,000,000 sterling at 6 per cent under imperial
edict and secured by the Maritime Customs. The firm replied
favorably, but Matheson and Company refused to touch any
loan sought by the Chinese government until the outcome of the
war had been determined.[75]

Chang Chih-tung was reported to have been empowered
to grant contracts in connection with the long-delayed Peking-
Hankow railroad which would be the first step in a comprehensive
program of economic and military development. Impressed,
Keswick hired Timothy Richard, a well-known missionary, described
as a close friend of the viceroy, to sound him out on this program, determine what would be needed, and send full reports to
Shanghai. Richard's first letter, written while negotiations
were in progress at Shimonoseki, confirmed that railroad building would begin as soon as practicable, the first section to run
from "opposite Chungkiang to Chingkiang-pei, a city on the Grand
Canal some fifty miles from Haichow, or from Nanking to the same
place, about three hundred miles."[76] The firm did not question
the advisability of organizing a railway system in the aftermath
of war and the program was taken as a sign that defeat had
mollified conservative opposition to long-delayed plans.[77]

Morrison prepared an engineering survey of the route and
Matheson and Company began inquiries about financing. The
taotai of Chinkiang assured the firm that the government would
build the railway as quickly as possible "by Imperial order"
with extensions to follow. He also told them that Chang Chih-
tung had been empowered to raise Tls. 5,000,000 for railroads,
the amount which he had requested of Jardine's a few weeks
earlier.[78]

Despite these signs of power and purpose at Nanking,
the Hong Kong Bank, possibly on the advice of the British
government, became an advocate of Hart's policy in the month of
the treaty: "They wish to discourage all loans except at Peking
where they hope to get an opportunity in the shape of an Indemnity Loan of thirty to fifty million Sterling."[79] Since
this contradicted what the firm had learned from Chang Chih-
tung, Keswick was skeptical: "Perhaps the big Indemnity Loan
at Peking is a very mythical matter for it would be far more
Chinese-like for the Central Government to permit or even order
provincial Viceroys (with the backing of Imperial Edicts) to raise
money as urgently required in sums of one or ten or more millions
partly in view of the Indemnity requirements and partly for defence or
development purposes."[80]

He also wrote that the whole indemnity was "only some
thirty million Sterling and only due by installments over seven
years," which meant that there would be no saving of interest
if the Peking government rushed to pay it off all at once; there
might be a loss since Japan had demanded only 5 per cent per
annum on installments due.[81]

Shortly after, Keswick wrote London that the firm would
be wise to cultivate Chang Chih-tung rather than follow the bank's
"central" policy because China lacked the national pride and
unity essential to strong central authority: "There is no public

to call for a speedy liquidation of the Indemnity." The humiliation of the central government or its regeneration would not
concern provincial governments. He also argued that the kind
of delay which central loans would entail might give China
some chance of escaping her obligations if, in time, "a
rupture occurred between Japan and Russia."[82]

A series of reports reinforced these ideas. They stated
that Li Hung-chang had been permanently discredited by China's
defeat, that the emperor and the court would probably retire
from Peking, and that there would be a new government led by
a "provincial faction" consisting of Chang Chih-tung, his
cousin Chang Chih-wan, and their followers. Sir Halliday
MacCartney's efforts to promote a big loan, on the suggestion
of Robert Hart, had reportedly been stopped by Chang whose wire
to Kung Chao-yuan, China's Minister in London, forbade such
activity. This was taken as further proof of the viceroy's
firm control of the government, and Keswick concluded that "so
long as Chang Chih-tung's party are so powerful it seems
impossible that any big consolidated loan will be arranged in
Pekin."[83]

Yet these reports were gradually disproved in the six
months following the treaty. Chang's faction did not become
dominant and negotiations for a large indemnity loan went
forward at Peking, not at Nanking, without any great change
in the administrative structure or any indication that a
central or a provincial party sought such change.

Realizing this, the firm acted to stay in the loan
field at Peking: "It is possible our name could be connected
with the Hong Kong and Shanghai Bank as joint agents issuing
any Loan and we will try to work on these lines through Sir
Robert Hart"--but the diverse political pressure behind what
became the £16,000,000 French-Russian loan and the tortuous

diplomacy preceding it, convinced Keswick that as an in-
dividual agency house they could no longer cultivate government business.[84] Partners agreed that some more formal
arrangement with the bank was needed, one which would provide for very close cooperation and a clear division of
spheres, the firm advancing the bank's financial agency while
the bank promoted their commercial interests. An ad hoc
arrangement of this kind had existed for years without having
been fully examined until the autumn of 1895 when both agreed
upon a set, though still non-contractual, policy of cooperation in the new era of national competition for the China
market.[85] Within three years their working arrangement took
legal form in the British and Chinese Corporation which became "the chosen instrument of the British Government" during
the subsequent battle of concessions.[86]

Confidence in the ultimate regeneration of China
through the conversion of its official class pervaded the
firm's correspondence until several months after the close
of the war with Japan. China's swift military collapse had
shaken this confidence severely without altogether destroying
it and some kind of government agency remained the primary
goal of the firm's relations with the bureaucracy. However,
Japan's victory had altered the character of the relationship.
Before the war ended, national rivalries which had been present, though muted, in the previous decade became clear; self-
strengthening had been exposed as a dangerous failure and the
future progress of Western enterprise in China seemed to
hinge upon the construction of a new modus vivendi, one founded
on the fact of China's administrative exhaustion.

CONCLUSION

The foregoing chapters of descriptive economic history indicate that Jardine, Matheson and Company, taken as representative
of major Western enterprise in late Ch'ing China, proved capable
of adapting to the special and changing circumstances of trade in
China, and they show that until Japan's aggression compounded its
inadequacies the high Ch'ing bureaucracy proved able to contain
and control Western enterprise whenever it threatened the tradi-
ional order.

The firm evolved from the status of agency house, investing
heavily in opium, to managing-agent and finally to managing-agent
and owner-investor, an evolution determined by a rational, often
cautious, response to conditions in China. As part of this response,
the firm showed a willingness to work closely with Chinese businessmen as long as they believed that these men might expand their
enterprise to match the opportunities available. When it became
evident that the strong recovery of China's internal commerce in
the late sixties and the widespread business activity of Chinese
merchants did not herald the birth of a new social order, that the
bureaucracy retained its command over the society and hence the
economy, Jardine's accepted these facts and sought profitable association with the traditonal elite.

Our perspective imposes some order upon relations between
Western firms, a small number of Chinese merchants, and a small
number of Chinese officials, yet for Jardine, Matheson and Company,
faced with the contemporary dilemmas of late nineteenth-century
China, economic decisions had to be empirical decisions controlled
by extraneous forces which directors of the firm often could not

understand. The firm employed comparatively little of its own
capital in productive enterprise in China--less than Tls. 5,000,000
at any time before 1895[1]--and emphasized safety of investment
consistently. When, after 1870, it made a sustained effort to assist
"economic development" in China, this cautious attitude remained,
though it did not prevent the offer of agency services, expert technical advice, and access to what was certainly the cheapest capital
available to the Chinese government.

Thus my reading of the Jardine papers does not produce
agreement with Nathan Pelcovitz's thesis that British firms in
China, Jardine's pre-eminently, thought "it was the function of the
government to open the whole of China as one vast Treaty Port, by
force and an occasional little war."[2] The papers will yield many
aggressive statements, especially in the inter-war decades, 1842-
1858, but these do not amount to a single fixed policy which advo-
cates continuous military pressure on China. For a generation,
from 1870 to 1895, policy statements found in the archive indicate
that members of the firm generally favored helping China to help
itself toward modernization. Aggressive views, the appeals of
frustrated businessmen for "an occasional little war," are rarely
found after the 1860's, though even these might be interpreted as
pro-Chinese in that they were concerned with the removal of
obstacles to economic growth rather than with assaults upon the
Chinese state as such. William Keswick did write that China in
1895 must not be treated too generously by Japan lest she forget the
lessons she had learned;[3] but this sort of thinking, the conviction
that the Ch'ing bureaucracy needed an awakening shock, hardly
justifies the conclusion that Western merchants were purposively
imperialist. The evidence of the Jardine archive will not support
any theory which assumes the imperialist character of Western

enterprise while postulating an utterly passive Chinese society as object of the aggression. On the contrary, the archive reveals that the most important Western firm in China sought partnership with China's ruling strata and found itself unable to dictate the terms of such partnership even in the context of China's progressive decline.

Jardine's experience over the first half-century of the treaty era indicates that whatever may have been the case after the late nineties, their over-all aim was the encouragement of a government-directed capitalism whose long-term development schemes would require every kind of profitable agency service, allowing the firm to work with pliant Chinese leaders and with a bureaucracy converted to policies which encouraged economic growth. Nicholas Kaldor has explained economic growth as a combination of population growth, capital accumulation, and technical progress, adding that: "They are manifestations of a process of development, but they cannot explain why the development occurs where it does when it does."[4] China had the growing population; it lacked technical innovations or a social order which would use them and it lacked the sort of social framework which would permit the use of accumulated capital in new ways. Jardine's and other Western firms tried, consciously and unconsciously, to break down traditional attitudes,[5] though they did not realize that a shift in traditional Chinese attitudes must entail the collapse of an entire social and political order. That Jardine's demonstration of the benefits of new kinds of investment, its offer of access to the latest in technical innovation and to capital, failed to stimulate significant economic change must be explained in terms of the nature of the traditional Chinese order, not in terms of economic imperialism[6] or the firm's failure to seek opportunities.

The second general conclusion which I belive the Jardine papers will allow is that the high Ch'ing bureaucracy understood the social threat of economic changes over which they could not retain absolute control. The bureaucracy proved able to defend its prerogatives until 1895 or later, using traditional devices to ensure that limited self-strengthening development remained under its direction. The Li Hung-chang group, even if one assumes that all its members had a single purpose, accepted a very narrow program of economic change by contrast with Meiji Japan, and it is clear that there was no acceptance within this group of what would have been the basis of a balanced, integrated, and industrialized economy. Indeed, there was no concept of national need apart from the need to strengthen the position of a bureaucratic faction. Even the most rational of the bureaucrats could not be expected to favor an economic program whose logical end, in disturbing the already shaken social order, would be to endanger the traditional agrarian base of all economic and political power in China. Thus the overtures to modernization, the arsenals, steamships, mines, and railways had to be organized in a manner (kuan-tu shang-pan) which assured conventional bureaucratic control. In the end, corruption and mismanagement prevented these projects from developing into a modern leading sector of the economy of China.

Thus, the firm's encouragement of the bureaucracy's limited self-strengthening program and its failure to understand the nature of official resistance to purely economic reasoning reflects a process of social interaction which does not lend itself to sweeping interpretations. Western enterprise in late Ch'ing China was an important and disruptive, but clearly subordinate factor within the framework of China's own complex evolution.

APPENDIX A

THE JARDINE MATHESON ARCHIVE
(Cambridge University Library)

Section of Accounts (Materials ranging from 1790's
through early 1900's)

Ledgers	94 vols.
Journals	170 vols.
Cash Books	90 vols.
Accounts Current	100 vols. (approximate)
Accounts Sales	156 vols.
Invoice Books	64 vols.

Miscellaneous papers comprising account books of
subsidiaries of Jardine, Matheson and Company; opium,
tea and silk freight books; lists of cargoes, manifests,
diaries. 600 vols. (approximate)

Loose papers and unbound materials containing general
accounts, invoices, bills, checks, estimates, receipts
and shipping lists, roughly sorted.   286 boxes

Correspondence (1814 to early 1900's)

Unbound Correspondence:

Incoming	65,000 letters (approximate)
Local	72,000 letters (approximate)
Japan/Korea	(no estimate)
Private	10,000 letters (approximate)

Letter Books:

India	67 vols.
Europe	58 vols.
Coastal	29 vols.
Local	12 vols.
Miscellaneous	64 vols.
Private	42 vols.
Insurance	26 vols.

Press Copy Letter Books	218 vols.
Hand-copies of Originals	78 vols.
Telegram Books	16 vols.
Unbound Duplicates	138 boxes

Prices Current and Market Reports	100 vols. and boxes
Unsorted Documents	13 boxes
Diaries	2 (1832-1833)
Chinese Documents	1 box

The Jardine, Matheson Archive has been catalogued by Miss
Norah Bartlett.

APPENDIX B*

INSURANCE AND BANKING

In keeping with the general evolution of larger China houses after the early sixties, Jardine's found that insurance and banking grew, like shipping, to be among the firm's most vital functions. In insurance the firm acted as agent for as many as eight companies,[1] though its chief interest, and largest investment, continued to rest in the Canton Insurance Office whose origins lie in the earliest days of the opium trade. In 1857 the firm opened a Chinese branch of the office in Shanghai and in Hong Kong, to serve the growing number of Chinese merchants who wanted the security of Western ships for their goods. The branch prospered; receipts for many months indicate a larger sale of policies among Chinese than among Western merchants, and quite often the Western branch of the office also sold policies to Chinese.[2]

In the late sixties the firm sought Chinese investment in the Canton Insurance Office. A European shareholder in Hong Kong, whose efforts on behalf of the company had been too slight, was informed that: "the competition to which our Insurance business is now exposed renders it necessary that we should only place shares where active support of our Canton office will be obtained. Therefore, three of your seven shares are to be given to influential Chinese in the North who can greatly assist the Office with coast risks, which are our best."[3] In the two companies which Jardine's controlled, the Canton Office and the Hong Kong Fire Insurance Company (founded in 1866), the number of Chinese shareholders increased in the seventies.[4] An announced issue of one hundred new shares

*For abbreviations used in Notes to Appendices, see p. 155.

in the Canton Office, because of the "great development of
trade in the East," had a provision reserving two-thirds
instead of one-third of the profits for distribution among
contributing shareholders, an innovation which attracted the
investments of seven "reputable Chinese" in Shanghai.[5] Such
joint-investment in insurance companies was another sign of
growing Chinese commercial strength and of Western attempts
to harness it in the sixties.

Jardine's had also performed rudimentary banking
services, for itself and others, from the earliest days of
trade. Large cash profits on opium allowed the firm
to settle and facilitate exchange in the years prior to the
opening of India-based Western banks on the China coast, and
opium profits had also left a reserve for business in advances
and loans.

Prior to treaty days the firm had lent large sums to
members of the Cohong (the Consoo Fund system guaranteeing
repayment with interest) which supported their indispensable
allies in trade, and provided good returns, often at very
high rates. Although the firm never committed such large
amounts at one time in post-treaty loans to Chinese merchants,
there were few seasons after 1842 in which some Jardine
Matheson and Company capital was not on loan to Chinese merchants.

In the forties and fifties the amounts were small, the
loans normally short-term, usually an advance to opium dealers
or business loans to the firm's compradores and, through them,
to provincial officials.[6] But, as the number of warehouses
and receiving hulks increased with the development of shipping,
the firm began a large business in advances on goods stored
in their godowns, particularly at Shanghai. This led naturally
to an extensive business in loans at the major ports and to
the investment of funds, through compradores, in a few

reputable and guaranteed "money shops" which returned much higher interest than that obtainable within the Western business community.[7]

In 1863 the Shanghai office established its own bank, the Ewo Bank, which arranged financing for exports and loans to Chinese merchants; the prevailing rate of interest with the Chinese community was never much below 12 per cent per annum, so that the firm was able to use all of its available capital by setting their rates 3 per cent to 5 per cent below the domestic rate.[8] Among the accounts of the Ewo Bank there are loans for large amounts ($260,000 to "Lee Hing" for three months at 8 per cent) but the majority were small sums for short periods,[9] William Keswick, who acted as manager of the bank, pointed out the value of timely loans as a means of "favourably influencing prominent men among the natives" and of predisposing them to do business with the firm.[10]

Most ambitious of the firm's financial development schemes was the proposal for a Bank of China to be founded in partnership with London associates and with Li Hung-chang and other high Chinese officials. Its outline had been explained to Li in November, 1883 (when there were rumours of war with France) by Alexander Michie who was also in communication with important Chinese bankers. The Bank of China would make a permanent loan to the Chinese government at easy interest; in return, the imperial government would grant the bank a monopoly of government business, including the financing of railway and mining development, and the power to issue notes which would be accepted for duties. Michie believed that negotiations about the bank were fostering Jardine's plans for control of the China Merchants, assuming

that any firm related so closely to government finances
would certainly be favoured as managing agents of state
shipping.[11]

     In August, 1884, after Jardine's had negotiated a
large loan to the imperial government, in the month when the
French fleet attacked Formosa and Foochow, the bank scheme
was still under discussion. Li told Michie he favored the
idea, but would wait until a more propitious time to raise
the matter in Peking. It continued to be mentioned as a
possibility for several years although there is no indication
that it was being considered very seriously in Peking.
(A telegram from Matheson and Company, April 24, 1885, stated:
"in the absence of special privileges we are of opinion
native bank cannot succeed in London".)

Notes to Appendix B

1. The Canton Insurance Office, the Hong Kong Fire Insurance
   Company, the Union Insurance Society of Canton, the Triton
   Insurance Company, the Bombay Insurance Company, the Bengal
   Insurance Society, the Ocean Marine Insurance Company of
   Bombay and the North China Insurance Company. See Accounts,
   Journals, May 1873. In 1860 there was only one local insurance company in China, the Canton. By 1870, there were
   six more. There was a purely Chinese company associated with
   the China Merchants. See Commercial Reports, China, No. 1
   (1875-1876), Shanghai, p. 46. In 1873, the Jardine-managed
   Hong Kong Fire Insurance Company "had over a million dollars
   invested and bearing interest." China Mail (Feb. 14, 1873),
   p. 3.

2. Accounts, Sh., 1857, 1865.

3. PCLB, HK-local, Sept. 22, 1869.

4. L. Box. Sh-local, Apr. 1, 1874. No figures given.

5. Ibid.

6. Accounts, Sh., Cash Books, 1848, 1856. No details given.

7. The high price of money in nineteenth-century China made possible the intervention of foreign capital at prices below those current with the Chinese. If such loans had been long term or cheaper they might have accelerated commercialization of the traditional economy; however, loans to Chinese merchants were normally short term and sensitive to every move in the rate of interest; in an average month at Shanghai, some thirty loans were made with interest varying from a few mace to 20 per cent per annum. As an example: "Hung Ching-Kung Tls. 3,000, at 10 per cent on security 100 packages of Nankins stored in Ewo West Godown"). In the same month, advances totaling Tls. 65,000 at 20 per cent had been made to fifteen Chinese hongs or individuals storing goods in "Hunt's Wharf," Tls. 11,000 at 15 per cent to Chinese under "Silk Advances," and loans to Chinese Banks in Shanghai totaled Tls. 24,000 at 2 1/2 mace per diem per tael.
The aim of the firm was also to compete with foreign banks anxious to lend surplus funds or "call money," as one letter stated: "Keep funds available in Shanghai for wharf advances. During this last ten weeks I could easily have got from twenty to thirty per cent with good security. There were numerous applications for advances on silk, tea and opium and also for advances at the wharves. Banks are anxious to get this business; we may lose it if we do not accommodate people." See Accounts, Apr. 1, 1874, and L. Box, Sh-HK, Sept. 28,1875.

8. L. Box, Sh-local, June 22, 1865.

9. Accounts, Sh, "Ewo Bank." 1865.

10. L. Box, Sh-Hk., Oct. 14, 1864. Business of this kind partly explains the firm's opposition to the founding of the Hong Kong and Shanghai Bank, with whom, even after members of the firm sat upon its board, Jardine's found itself in close competition for thirty years. The Ewo Bank closed in 1867 upon the failure of Ekee, a Shanghai silk merchant who had been its principal investor. The Ewo Bank was a "native bank" founded by Jardine,Matheson and Company in cooperation with Ekee.

11. L. Box, Tientsin-Sh, to W. Paterson, Dec. 5, 1883.

12. L. Box, HK-Sh, to W. Paterson, quoting telegram from F.B. Johnson, London, Apr. 24, 1885.

APPENDIX C

KOREA

In the years after 1870 the firm placed new emphasis upon
Japan accounts and had begun to explore alternative business
opportunities in East Asia. A report on tin mines at Selangor,
Malaya, had been requested in April, 1884, in order to ascertain
their value as a possible investment.[1] When Von Mollendorf
(of the customs service, appointed by Li Hung-chang as advisor
to the king of Korea) requested Tls. 500,000 on behalf of the
Korean government in January, 1883, the firm replied that they
could not consider a loan until they had had more experience of
the country. Six months later the king had granted the firm an
exclusive mining concession in Northwest Korea; an agency had
opened in Seoul to supervise exploration of the concession;
the firm had given a contract to carry tribute rice on a Jardine
steamer from the southern ports to Seoul; and Keswick was
considering Harry Parkes' suggestion that a company be formed
to build a railway from Inchon (Chemulpo) to Seoul: "by
working with the Korean Government in these undertakings we
shall have first refusal of the railway."[2]

The most interesting point about the firm's effort to
"open" Korea was the persistent demand made for Korean government participation in each project. Unwilling to bear the cost
of a possibly fruitless mining survey the firm had asked the
king for "closest cooperation and a free supply of men" and when
neither was forthcoming they began to lose interest in Korean
gold[3] because: "we did not at the outset fully realize the
magnitude of the work we were undertaking in Corea...an
expensive survey of the Kingdom at our own cost. Even if we

should eventually find a mine with gold in paying quantity we should have to expend a large capital and to contend with all the difficulties raised by obstructive officials and a very inapt people."[4]

In the autumn of 1884 the Seoul agency was closed though Von Mollendorf was assured that the firm would resume in Korea if agents of the government would cooperate and entrepreneurial risks were carefully measured.

H. W. Beecher, who had been employed by Jardine's as their mining engineer from early 1884, inspected and reported on four distinct and widely separated localities which the firm had hopes of developing. One report dealt with Malaya, one Korea, and two with China. Beecher said: "The result of my labours being only to find that none of these places were of sufficiently assured value to enable me to advise you to enter on immediate active mining operations." The reports on Malaya and Korea described collateral disadvantages independent of the probable value of mineral deposits. A number of mining enterprises had recently failed in Malaya because of "mis-representation and mis-management" while Korea,"ill fated and poverty stricken," was, as Jardine's had recently discovered, unsuitable for investment without government guarantees. The China surveys had been made under the direction of Gustav Detring and they too advised against investment in the areas (unnamed) surveyed. Beecher recommended a policy of cautious prospecting rather than a "rash commencement of great undertakings."[5]

Notes to Appendix C

1. UC, HK-Sh., to W. Paterson, Apr. 17, 1884. There is also mention of a Matheson & Company report "on Tong King-sing's Yangtze copper ore which is more satisfactory. The deposit is worth prospecting and securing by him and we should endeavor to be in safe manner connected with it." I find no further mention of the matter in this series of letters.

2. PLB, Sh-HK., to W. Keswick, May 28, 1884. Apparently there was considerable ill feeling between British diplomats and employees of the Imperial Maritime Customs. Parkes accused Von Mollendorf of overrating his influence with the king and of "talking in the wildest way about his arrangement with Jardine Matheson being sanctioned by the Legation in Peking." The firm had obtained the concession through Von Mollendorf: "We have a proper agreement with the Corean government through Von M."

3. Keswick had asked Paterson about the possible sale of piece goods in Korea; the latter replied that "there is the problem of returns." Ibid. William Gubbins, Jardine's agent, warned the firm against becoming involved with the Korean government: "...the government are a set of squeezes worse than any Chinese yamen. They have opened the country unwillingly and not content with the usually adopted plundering are resolved to steal by any means they can and make a so-called agreement a further means of doing so. The government are entirely to blame for the state of the country present and past, and it's only to be hoped that they get no private assistance in the form of a loan." UC, Korea, 1883-1884, to W. Paterson, Sh. July 21, 1883. Later J.J. Keswick wrote to an agent at Chemulpoo (Inchon) that if the Korean government entered the foreign money market for a loan their security would be judged insufficient: "I do not think we will seriously consider a loan to Korea." UC, Sh-Korea, to B.A. Clarke, May 16, 1884.

4. PLB, Sh-HK, to W. Keswick, Aug. 9, 1884, Keswick had received instructions from Robert Jardine of Matheson and Company, "to close as early as possible all direct interest in mining be it at Selungor or in Corea...the Corean government should take over our mining interest there," which indicates that Matheson and Company had full control of Jardine's mining investment behavior.

5. UC, Sh-local, Dec. 10, 1886.

APPENDIX D

KEROSENE

The seventies and early eighties were years of relative
stagnation in China trading, years in which Chinese demand for
the traditional staples of the import trade seemed to have
reached its upper limit.[1] During these years, therefore,
Jardine's and others experimented with miscellaneous imports
ranging from iron rods to mirrors, but only one of these,
kerosene oil, became a major trade item and changed ancient
ways throughout China. The firm sold small amounts of Russian
oil, carried via Suez, at Shanghai in the early seventies.
This oil did not, to any great extent, replace vegetable oils
normally used for lighting because its price was not yet
competitive. Yet imports grew, reaching 250,000 gallons by 1880.

The oil was concentrated at Shanghai and was distributed
by Chinese dealers to nearby villages and up the Yangtze.
Lamps had been expensive until, in 1882, a cheap lamp was
produced by Chinese manufacturers at Canton and sold at a price
which could be met by millions. This innovation created new
demand, raising imports from 384,000 gallons in 1883, to
839,000 in 1884. A report stated: "The chief portion...is
due to provincial demand, 511,770 gallons having been sent into
the interior under transit pass (1/2 of import duty), of which
380,780 gallons were sent by Chinese. The above facts are
remarkable as showing no prejudice against the foreign origin
of any article will prevent a ready sale, provided its price,
quality and general utility show it is adapted to the wants
and purses of the most numerous class of consumer."[2]

Jardine's began to import American oil in 1881 and handled smaller consignments of Sumatran oil from 1883. In the mid-eighties the firm was anticipating growing demand and had imported as much as 380,000 gallons per annum on joint-account with "Ching Chang" (possibly Cheng Kuan-ying), a Shanghai businessman, whose hold on the kerosene market in China was usually unchallenged in the eighties and nineties.[3] The firm also acted as agent for the American Tidewater Company, a Standard Oil associate, through whom they placed most orders.

Early in 1890 John Macgregor considered importing refined oil from the Pacific coast of the United States in a fleet of rented tank-steamers; the plan was dropped because Ching Chang would not cooperate. He had the greater part of his capital locked in kerosene at the time.[4] As an alternative the firm joined partners of Matheson and Company in organizing The London & Pacific Petroleum Company which was intended to develop oil-bearing property in Peru, market the oil first in Peru and Chile, then come into the rising China market with, they believed, highly competitive prices. The board sat in London for the first time in March 1890 and one thousand shares were offered at £10 per share. The Shanghai community took 200 and 50 per cent was taken by Ching Chang, Ho Tung (a J.M. & Co. compradore) and associates. Judging from the scant correspondence, oil was actually produced between 1890 and 1894 and sold in Peru, but costs had been much higher than anticipated, dividends impossible, and none of the London and Pacific Petroleum Company's oil reached China. The enterprise was liquidated in January, 1894.[5]

In 1893 Jardine's made their major bid for agency control of oil distribution in China by offering to become agents for both Standard Oil and Tidewater throughout Asia in return for

146

the managing agency of Standard's new Sumatra concessions: "The firm's interest in kerosene is now quite a full one. We have particulars of the Sumatra oil and mineral concessions. The Standard Oil surveyors are satisfied and have made an agreement with the Sultan. The Capital of the proposed Company will be £250,000 in 50,000 shares of £5 each...if we agree it will be a condition that Jardine Matheson & Co. shall be in Sumatra the permanent managers of the Co. under, of course, the control of the Board of Directors and that a member of the firm shall be a Director in London." Beyond this, Jardine, Matheson and Company would be permanent agents for the Standard Sumatra Company in the Netherlands, India, Singapore and the Straits, Siam, Annam, Cochin-China, Tonkin, Hong Kong, China, Japan, and the Philippines; their commission as managers and agents was to be 3 per cent on all sales.[6]

After nine months of negotiation the Standard Oil Company informed the firm that despite its excellent management of Tidewater interests in China and Japan, they had decided to establish their own marketing organization in Asia. Keswick wrote: "This squeezes us out of the trade unless we can become representative of either the other American or the Russian combination." However, Standard's decision meant Jardine's exclusion from the trade as major importers or consignees on American account. Russian oil was not an attractive alternative, either in terms of its price or its availability in China: "American organization has in great measure destroyed the Russian Oil business in Western Europe and has a certain hold in India, China and Japan..."[7]

Notes to Appendix D

1. See Yang Tuan-liu, Table 5, p. 20.

2. Commercial Reports, China, No. 2 (1884), p. 87.

3. CLB, HK-Coast, to J.M. & Co., Sh., Aug. 7, 1883 and Apr. 19, 1884.

4. Ibid., May 9, 1890.

5. UC, London & Pacific Petroleum Co., March 1890-January 1894. Macgregor wrote that J.M. & Co. had more money than it could usefully employ in February 1890. See PLB, HK-Sh., Feb. 11, 1890.

6. PLB, Sh-HK., to J. Macgregor, Apr. 12, 1893.

7. One volume, W. Keswick, London, to G.L. Montgomery, N.Y., Mar. 31, 1894, Apr. 14, 1894.

APPENDIX E

THE EXPORT TRADE

As with opium and cotton, the firm's experience with the
great export staples of the China trade, tea and silk, demonstrated its ability to respond to conditions in the new ports
as well as within the Chinese economy, even when these were not
clearly understood. In the 1840's and 1850's the firm profited
from the financing of exports because many Western firms without
large capital in China would accept advances from Jardine's in
order to pay for their tea and silk, leaving their London
correspondent to repay the loan to Matheson and Company, usually
within ninety days. The firm preferred this means of remittance
since it removed the element of risk attendant upon their own
investment in an uncertain market.[1] Chinese merchants, who had
contracted in the interior for tea coming forward to a stagnant
market, were also attracted by an offer of cheap credit and the
opportunity to enter the export trade on their own account. Many
accepted Jardine loans during the 1846-1847 season. These enabled
them to meet debts due on customary settling dates and led to
piece goods orders through Jardine's, purchased with proceeds
realized in London by Matheson and Company.[2] Such cooperation
in exports was a fairly rare arrangement in the forties, but in
1851 Jardine's began to ship teas regularly on joint-account with
"a reputable Shanghai Hong" (Mau Foong Hong) which included
Cantonese merchants known to the firm in the opium trade. Their
Shanghai manager negotiated the business through Ahee, the firm's
chief Shanghai "tea man." The aim seems to have been to ensure
that tea ships from Foochow and Canton would be well filled when
the firm was not inclined to invest or had insufficient orders.

This practice went on intermittently through the fifties, diminishing as exports grew in volume and home prices made agency business steadier and more profitable.

Export volumes grew so rapidly in the fifties that direct purchases by the agents of foreign firms could not have amounted to more than one-fifth or one-sixth of tea sales in the producing areas, though the prices in these areas were probably used as a guide to the whole trade. Western merchants had ceased to rely entirely upon tea brokers at Canton and Shanghai in the late forties. Their own buyers, supplied with silver dollars, went into the tea districts of Fukien, Kiangsi and up the Yangtze; this may have been an important factor in shifting the tea routes away from trade channels which were not so much "natural" as embedded in the traditional interests and privileges which had grown up around the Canton System for decades.[3]

However, it was basically cooperation with Chinese merchants which gave the firm a fuller knowledge of crop conditions and prices in China than would otherwise have been possible at that time. Western merchants knew as much as Robert Fortune had published in his books about the general working of trade, yet they needed continuous and accurate information about crops and prices to guide agents at Foochow and Canton. After the first shipments had been purchased by a firm's Chinese tea buyers in the country, it was usual to make further purchases from Chinese brokers at the ports, depending upon advices from London and the out-turn of the first teas, and these further purchases were made on the basis of estimates of available supplies and prices prevailing in the country districts.[4] Fortune had calculated that Chinese merchants buying in Fukien and shipping to Shanghai made an average profit of Tls. 8 per picul, net, after paying

one-half that amount to the tea farmers.[5] In 1856, George
Fisher, the firm's Foochow agent reported the departure of
Ahu, Russell and Company's tea buyer, for the tea districts
with a Western employee of the firm who intended to "go about
and see the different Hongs and the process of preparing tea,
disguised as a Chinaman."[6] In March of that year Ahee, Jardine's
tea buyer, reported that he had purchased 3000 chests of first
crop teas at Tls. 18 per picul from village brokers in the
"Sin Chune Kai" area of Fukien, on the slopes of the famed
Bo-hea hills. Transport and Chinese customs were expected to
be about Tls. 7 per picul (approximately one chest) from this
area to Foochow, and he promised delivery at Foochow within
two weeks from the date of his letter.[7] It is interesting to
compare this report with the prices and charges described by
Fortune six years earlier, before the Taiping rebellion had
got underway and when the volume of tea exported was 40 per
cent smaller: in 1849, Chinese merchants had purchased the
finest teas in what appears to have been the same general
area for Tls. 8 per picul. Transport and customs charges
came to about Tls. 14 per picul for teas traveling some 500
miles from Fukien to Shanghai, where they sold to the Western
merchant for about Tls. 22 per picul. In 1856 the Chinese
agent, acting for a Western firm, purchased fine teas for Tls.
18 per picul and charges were expected to be about Tls. 7 per
picul from northwest Fukien to Foochow, a distance of some
200 miles.

If these figures are representative they show that the
primary cost of tea had at least doubled between 1849 and 1856
and that transport costs had remained steady, unaffected by the
new likin taxes (or the movements of the rebels in 1855-1856).
This suggests one reason why agents were employed in the tea

districts, despite the risks involved, but it does not explain
why foreign merchants also continued to buy large quantities
from Chinese brokers at Foochow, unless it is assumed that the
Chinese were now content to receive lower profits than previously.

Silk exports ran to the same pattern. The business was
centered at Shanghai, adjacent to the important Tsatlee and
Tay-Saam silk-producing areas of South Kiangsu and North
Chekiang, although Canton, drawing upon silk areas of Southwest
Kwangtung, continued to hold an important share of the trade
during these years. The firm had recognized silk's potential
value as an export before 1840 and tea ships had carried
consignments of "Nankin" silk from Canton[8] during the thirties.
Later, heavy investment and close relations with Chinese brokers
whose functions often included both opium smuggling and export
organization (that is, buying and transporting tea from Hankow,
contracting for silk cloth in the Shanghai hinterland) carried
the firm into the front rank of silk exporters at Shanghai.
Accounts of 1846-1847 debit $1,474,341.00 for "raw silk to England"
(Mainly "Nankin" from Canton), and accounts of 1853-1854 show
increases -- to $2,050,000.00 -- which indicate that the Taiping
were not at that time preventing export of silk surpluses. As
agents for Matheson and Company's accounts and an increasing
number of foreign firms, Jardine's handled over two million dollars
in raw silk annually through the fifties, except in 1858 when the
accounts list half that value.[9]

The firm did not attempt to send their own agents to the
silk districts. Purchases took place at Canton and Shanghai, a
difference from tea policy which may be attributed to the relative
nearness of the silk districts and the fact that transport and
other charges were moderate. A European traveling in the
Shanghai hinterland (North Chekiang) in 1848 reported: "the

cost of production was nearly equal to the prices paid in Shanghai for raw silk."[10] Fortune, in 1852, reported from the same area: "The quantity exported bears but a small proportion to that consumed by the Chinese themselves and the 17,000 extra bales sent yearly out of the country have not in the least degree affected the price of raw silk or of silk manufactures. This fact speaks for itself."[11]

As pointed out in Chapter III, the gradual restoration of order in the producing districts in the sixties, the opening of the Yangtze to foreign shipping and the interior to foreign merchants, the continuous rise in volume of tea exports apparently without fundamental change in the traditional methods of production and marketing, the temporary disappearance of silk as a large trade item and its reappearance at the end of the decade, and the impact of improved communications with European and American markets all affected China's exports. Dealing in tea and silk became much more competitive and less profitable to an agent.

Tea business remained precarious through the seventies and the firm did not demur when the Koenigsberg Commercial Association, in 1881, commented: "it has been apparent for some time the Indian teas have shown better value than the China growths, also that the quantity shipped to this country has increased every year and that they have begun to drive the China teas out of the market."[12] Similar conditions applied to silk, about which the firm had become equally pessimistic, condemning speculation and complaining that profits for investors through the seventies and early eighties were unsatisfactory. In silk, Chinese firms were as involved as foreigners and suffered as much when overstocked European markets broke several firms in 1877. The effects of Chinese failures upon foreign houses were equally severe.[13]

In silk also there was an effort to combine among foreign merchants who in 1879 and 1880 refused to buy until home markets had cleared. But it had no success.[14]

As a consequence of so much unsatisfactory business the firm placed renewed emphasis upon influencing Chinese and foreign shippers to use their steamship and insurance services for tea and silk and upon loans to merchants storing silk in their godowns. Thus in exports also the firm found itself increasingly concerned with servicing trade and with seeking new business opportunities appropriate to the changed economic conditions of the seventies.

Notes to Appendix E

1. CLB, to A.G. Dallas, Sept. 7, 1847.
2. UC, London, Aug. 23, 1847.
3. J.M. & Co. was ambivalent about the "Canton Interest." There are references to the advantage of concentrating export business at Canton or Shanghai. See UC, HK-Canton, Dec. 9, 1845.
4. CLB, to A.G. Dallas, Apr. 14, 1851. Also CLB, HK-Sh, July 8, 1855.
5. R. Fortune, A Journey to the Tea Countries of China (London, 1852), pp. 268-269.
6. UC, Foochow, G. Fisher, May 18, 1856.
7. UC, Foochow, G. Fisher, Mar. 9, 1856. Another advantage of employing tea buyers lay in the Western merchant's consequent power to specify certain types and qualities of tea for purchase on his own account, instead of being compelled to accept kinds offered by Chinese merchants.
8. Manifests, Canton, 1839-1940.
9. See Ledgers HK, 1846-1847, 1853-1854 and other volumes in series for the 1850's.
10. Scarth, p. 13.

11. Fortune, Journey to the Tea Countries, p. 28.

12. UC, London, K.C.A. to J.M. & Co., HK., Mar. 15, 1881. See also China Mail (HK) Sept. 16, 1877, which says that the amount of China tea consumed in England had been stationary since 1876. The writer blames the decline upon "the primitive methods of preparation in China."

13. Commercial Reports, China, No. 1 (1879), Shanghai, p. 5.

14. Ibid.

NOTES

Abbreviations Used in the Notes

BPP	British Parliamentary Papers
CLB	Coastal Letter Book
ELB	Europe Letter Book
HK	Hong Kong
ILB	India Letter Book
IMC	China, Imperial Maritime Customs
J.S. & Co.	Jardine, Skinner and Company
M & Co.	Matheson and Company, London
PCLB	Press Copy Letter Book
PLB	Private Letter Book
SA:AC	Section of Accounts, Accounts Current
UC	Unbound Correspondence in Letter Box
UC:L	Unbound Correspondence, Local
UC:Pr	Unbound Correspondence, Private

Introduction

1. A.J. Sargent, Anglo-Chinese Commerce and Diplomacy (Oxford, 1907) is carefully detailed. H.B. Morse, The Trade and Administration of China, rev. ed. (Shanghai, 1913). See also John K. Fairbank, Alexander Eckstein and L.S. Yang, "Economic Change in Early Modern China: An Analytic Framework," Economic Development and Cultural Change (October 1960).

2. Michael Greenberg, in British Trade and the Opening of China, 1800-1842, p. 13, estimates the total value of China's foreign trade at £9,625,138 in 1828. R.M. Martin, in China: Political, Commercial and Social (London, 1847), II, 148, mentions a total value of £11,100,000 for 1842. S. Osborn, in The Past and Future of British Relations in China (London, 1860), pp. 13, 104, estimating roughly on the basis of

Shanghai figures speaks of £30,200,000 total value in 1857. China, Imperial Maritime Customs, Reports on Trade at the Treaty Ports, 1870, 1880, show £35,254,412 for 1870, £46,278,371 for 1880. A. Krausse, China in Decay (London, 1900), p. 252. The figure based upon the "Foreign Office return," is £55,600,000.

3. Robert Hart, These From the Land of Sinim: Essays on the Chinese Question (London, 1903), p. 60; and John K. Fairbank, Trade and Diplomacy on the China Coast: The Opening of the Treaty Ports, 1842-1854 (Cambridge, Mass., 1953), p. 288.

4. Commercial Reports of Her Majesty's Consuls in China, China, No. 3 (1872), Foochow.

5. Ssu-yü Teng, New Light on the History of the Taiping Rebellion (Cambridge, Mass., 1950), pp. 18, 43. In 1830 one tael of silver equalled 1000 copper coins; in 1848, 2000 coins; in 1851, 4900 coins.

6. Confirmed by A. Reid, Matheson and Company, in a private letter, Nov. 6, 1957. I have been unable to answer these questions: What were the general or administrative costs of a large China firm? What was Jardine Matheson and Company's net profit in a given year? Were profits normally reinvested in the treaty ports or remitted to London for investment abroad? Did Matheson and Company have a veto over the "Head in the East," although control was formally in Hong Kong?

7. Matheson and Company, Ltd., London, was founded in 1848 as a private house of merchant bankers by James Matheson who had left China in 1842. Each firm described the other as a foreign representative. Matheson and Company is today controlled by Jardine, Matheson and Company, Hong Kong. See Fairbank, Trade and Diplomacy, Vol. 2, Appendix A, pp. 56-57, for a partial list of Jardine Matheson and Company's most important nineteenth-century partners. The heads of J.M. & Co., Hong Kong & China, for the period 1842-1895 were:

Alexander Matheson	1842-1852
David Jardine	1852-1856
Joseph Jardine	1856-1860
Alexander Perceval	1860-1864
James Whittall	1864-1874
William Keswick	1874-1886
John MacGregor	1886-1893
James Keswick	1893-1895

8. R.C. North, in the historical commentary and notes on Hsiao
    Yü, Mao Tse-tung and I were Beggars (Syracuse, N.Y., 1959),
    p. 212. Robert Hart had a similar opinion of Western
    aggressiveness. See his These From the Land of Sinim, pp.
    69, 82, 163.

I. The Opium Trade

1. Tu Lien-che, "Lin Tse-hsu," in A.W. Hummel, ed., Eminent
    Chinese of the Ch'ing Period, 1644-1912 (Washington, 1943-
    1944), I, 511.

2. H.B. Morse, The Trade and Administration of the Chinese
    Empire (Shanghai, 1913) pp. 339, 340, mentions Tls. 10,000,000
    but doubts that the annual export from China was so large.

3. China, Imperial Maritime Customs, Treaties, Conventions,
    etc. between China and Foreign States, Misc. Series, No. 30,
    Vol. 1, 2nd ed. (Shanghai: Inspectorate General of Customs,
    1917). See pp. 351-390 for texts of the Treaty of Nanking
    and supplementary treaties.

4. See Fairbank, Trade and Diplomacy, "The Opium Settlement of
    1843," Chap. 9, pp. 133-151.

5. See correspondence in The Chinese Repository, 16:44 (1847).

6. G.B. Endacott, The History of Hong Kong (Oxford, 1958), p. 73.

7. UC:Pr, Sh., January to September 1865, Apr. 8, 1865. Other
    references to the prosperity of the opium trade during periods
    of slow trading are found in PLB, HK. to India, May 12, 1846,
    and ibid., Sh. local, Apr. 2, 1873.

8. Fairbank, Trade and Diplomacy, p. 287.

9. See D.E. Owen, British Opium Policy in China and India (New
    Haven and London, 1934), pp. 18-48, 80-112, and Morse, Trade
    and Administration, p. 352. "Shipment of Indian Opium to
    China." See Sargent, pp. 127, 132, 212. Jardine, Matheson
    and Company listed the export of Malwa Opium to China as
    1850: 29,582 chests; 1855: 48,390 chests; 1860: 17,665
    chests; 1865: 41,883 chests; 1870: 40,020 chests;
    1875: 38,786 chests (Unbound correspondence, India, 1876,n.d.)

10. R.M. Martin asserts that Jardine, Matheson and Company partners shared "three million sterling in twenty years ...Much the larger portion of the sum was amassed within the last ten years (1837-1847) and the profits of that house now, far exceed those of any former period." II, 258.

11. See ELB, 1846-1849, from HK. for comments on the lack of demand for British piece goods.

12. BPP, Report from the Select Committee of the Commons on Commercial Relations with China, with Minutes of Evidence, (1847), Vol. 5.

13. See Osborn, pp. 103-109, for a tendentious summary of these arguments. Also, Rutherford Alcock, Consular Report from Foochow, June 1845, reprinted in F.E. Forbes, Five Years in China (London, 1848), Appendix VI, p. 341. Alcock wrote that "a trader of reputed substance and respectability affirmed, in conversations, that the trade of the port had considerably decreased during the last few years, which he attributed to the 'drain of capital, in the best of times not very plentiful, caused by the opium traffic...immense sums...which would otherwise have been invested in a more legitimate and profitable commerce.'" p. 343. Martin quotes the taotai of Shanghai to the same effect, II, 258. See also The Chinese Repository (March 1843), p. 168.

14. See Sargent, p. 133 and Incoming Correspondence, LB London, 1854, from Hayter and Howell. London, Jan. 9, 1854. Beginning in 1851, at least £1,000,000 in silver bullion had been exported from England annually to China in part payment for tea and silk. See ILB, to Charles Skinner, Apr. 18, 1854.

15. BPP: Papers Relating to the Opium Trade in China, 1842-1856, Sess. 2, 1857, XLIII, 64.

16. PLB, A.M. to James Abel-Smith, Mar. 29, 1846.

17. ILB, to Charles Skinner, May 5, 1854.

18. ELB, to M & Co., Sept. 23, 1857.

19. Ibid.

20. See D. Torr, ed. "Marx on China, 1853-1860," Articles from The New York Daily Tribune (London, 1951), p. 3. Marx believed that imports of British cottons had caused social distress during the 1850's: "In China the spinners and weavers have suffered greatly under this foreign competition and the community have become unsettled in proportion." He was probably misled by India's experience with foreign manufactured goods.

21. See Box, Accounts Sh., 1854-1855.

22. J. Scarth, Twelve Years in China: The People, The Rebels
     and The Mandarins, by a British Resident, p. 117.
     (Edinburgh, 1860).

23. Sir Henry Pottinger was personally friendly to members of
     the firm and their reports to India and London included
     official information on Chinese and British attitudes
     toward the trade. The firm's knowledge of official Chinese
     attitudes was largely derived from Pottinger and it accords
     with diplomatic records. During most of 1843 Alexander
     Matheson believed there would be a resurgence of imperial
     determination to crush the opium trade by force of arms.
     There were also a number of false alarms about large
     Chinese military movements in various coastal areas, all
     derived either from Chinese staff or from dealers along
     the coast. A willingness to consider, if not to act upon
     such rumors, was characteristic of officials in the head
     office at Hong Kong for most of the century. ELB to James
     Abel-Smith, London, Nov. 15, 1843; CLB to A.G. Dallas, et.
     al., Apr. 2, 1843, Nov. 30, 1843.

24. PLB, A.M. to James Abel-Smith, London, Aug. 9, 1843, and
     CLB, June 12, 1843.

25. "Consul Balfour will give you as little trouble as he can
     but it is advisable to be as independent of him as possible
     ..." CLB to Opium receiving ships, Sept. 20, 1843. "We
     do not expect the consul to interfere with shipping outside
     the port of Amoy, so long, at all events, as they confine
     themselves to the sale of Opium." Ibid., Sept. 25, 1843.

26. PLB, A.M. to John Purvis, Singapore, Mar. 8, 1843.

27. PLB, A.M. To Jamsetjee Jeejeebhoy, Sept. 10, 1843. He
     wrote then "that if ever the trade is legalized, it will
     cease to be profitable from that time. The more difficulties
     attend it, the better for you and us."

28. Greenberg, p. 139 and CLB, July 16, 1842.

29. Greenberg, pp. 206-209, on trade during the war and
     fluctuations in the price of opium. Also, PLB, A.M. to
     James Abel-Smith, London, Sept. 6, 1842, which reads in
     part: "I wish that the war had lasted a few more years,
     as the opium trade did well and may now be curtailed."

30. Asiatic Journal, 26:537 (Calcutta, 1828).

31. Greenberg, pp. 136-141.

32. On the post-treaty coastal system see PLB, A.M. 1842-1843.
    Also The Chinese Repository (May 1844). "The growth of
    opium advances steadily; and so long as the demand from
    consumers remains unchecked, this production will
    doubtless continue annually to augment. In the papers of
    the day, we see the crop for the current year estimated
    at 22,000 of Bengal, and 26,000 of Malwa, making a total
    of 48,000 chests, which at $700 each will make a return
    of $33,600,000. And we see too, that his excellency Sir
    Henry Pottinger, at Bombay, has come out in favor of the
    trade in opium."

33. LB, to R.W. Crawford, Bombay, Oct. 14, 1844.

34. PLB, HK. to India, Mar. 5, 1846.

35. Greenberg, p. 164.

36. PLB, HK. to India, to Jamsetjee Jeejeebhoy, Aug. 18, 1846.
    R.M. Martin calculated an agent's profit on one chest of
    opium sold for $700 to be $113, apart from profit on
    insurance and freight. II, 258.

37. See R.M. Martin on the Canton Interest, II, 168-169.

38. PLB, HK. to India, to R.W. Crawford, Bombay, Apr. 9, 1846.
    In that month the firm had 1147 chests of Patna, 181 of
    Benares, and 1300 of Malwa stored on the coast and at Hong
    Kong. At the time, this constituted 2 1/2 months' supply.

39. W.T. Power, Recollections of Three Years Residence in
    China (London 1853), describes the working of the
    duopoly, pp. 112-115. Also CLB, HK. to ships and places
    on the China coast, 1842-1845.

40. See Power, p. 113.

41. The Extension of Peninsular and Oriental steamship services
    to the coast and their carriage of opium from 1850 broke
    the hold of the two large firms. See Fairbank, Trade and
    Diplomacy, pp. 238-239.

42. CLB, HK. to coast, 1842-1852, Vols. 1-5.

43. UC:L, HK., Aug. 9, 1851.

44. CLB, HK. to Commanders, May 29, 1851.

45. One series, from a Captain Roope at the estuary of the
    River Min, may be taken as typical. His reports are found
    in UC:L, Foochow and River Min, May 14, 1845 - June 11, 1847.

46. CLB, HK. to A.G. Dallas, Sh., June 4, 1852.

47. ILB, May 6, 1843 (See full list on p. 366) and ILB,
     1854-1855. The firm asked Jeejeebhoy "to continue your
     letters of introduction to sure friends."

48. H. Brown, Parry's of Madras (London, 1954), p. 99.

49. See Greenberg, p. 146.

50. (1) "What is the present amount of manufactured Opium
     on hand in the country (i.e. Rajputana and the Native States)?
     Reply: 2000 chests of old drug 1846/47 and about 9000 to
     10,000 of new 1847/48 now coming in. (2) Whether there is
     a prospect of extensive failure to the crop now sowing?
     Reply: the want of water will doubtless occasion a
     considerable reduction but the rates being so high it may
     be expected, and is, that every means will be taken, such
     as sinking fresh wells, to procure water. So suspicious,
     however, are those who make advances that they are waiting
     until the crop is high to see what water remains for the
     advancing stage of the poppy before they lend money. The
     crop cannot exceed 9000 or 10,000 chests, though ordinarily
     12,000. If there are high prices just before the rains they
     will adulterate to 12,000 but this Opium won't come in
     before November. The rule is...if prices are high, they
     adulterate, if low, store their drug." UC, Bombay, 1848, n.d.

51. ILB to Jamsetjee Jeejeebhoy, Sept. 7, 1848.

52. UC, Bombay, Apr. 2, 1847.

53. ILB to Jardine, Skinner and Company, Calcutta, Oct. 9,
     1852, July 15, 1854. See also Misc. Accounts, SA:AC
     with Jardine, Skinner and Company 1854-1855.

54. UC, Calcutta, Nov. 11, 1850. "Memo of Opium Cultivation,
     Behar Opium Agency, 11 November, 1850: For five days rain
     fell incessantly, which not only has retarded the sowings
     but has damaged them considerably and will necessitate the
     resowing of a large quantity of land. On the whole it will
     make the crop a late one which is objectionable, a late
     crop of poppy never being so plentiful as an early one."
     These reports went into great detail, reporting on each
     area in Behar.

55. ILB, to G.M. Robertson, Calcutta, Apr. 28, 1855.

56. An example of Jardine, Matheson and Company's joint-investment
     with India Houses: for the first six months of 1844 Jardine's
     share of opium shipments was $445,000 with Jeejeebhoy and
     Company, $330,000 with Remington and Company, and $443,000

with Jardine, Skinner and Company. In the same period
the firm invested approximately $1,372,980 on its own
account through these firms. In 1846-1847, a year more
typical of all import business in China between the wars,
the figures for joint-account investment in opium had
increased by a third or more. The importance of the
drug to each firm may also be seen in the remittance of
profits from China to London. Remington took bills on
London, unless the home market for Chinese produce was
very favorable, and used these funds to finance piece
goods shipments to India. Jardine, Skinner varied remittance.

Jeejeebhoy required remittance to London on both
opium and cotton and he would not allow it in any form
other than "good bills," or treasure. During periods
of money scarcity in China, Jardine's took large shipments
of tea, regardless of market conditions, in order to provide
Jeejeebhoy with funds in London. Ships' manifests also
show a steady growth of consignments made by smaller firms
through the three agents; when disinclined to invest on
their own account in a particular shipment, Jardine's
authorized advances to small shippers of amounts up to
three-quarters of Bombay value, thereby achieving closer
control over supplies. This enabled them to be firmer
when facing "the shrewd and far-sighted Chinese dealer."
Bulk sales had been their aim for years: "We shall always
find ways and means to carry on in spite of every obstacle
and the larger the proportion of the importations placed
under our management the better able shall we be to
support prices." UC, Bombay, Sept. 17, 1850; ILB, to
Jardine, Skinner and Company, Calcutta, May 4, 1850; PLB,
A.M. to Jamsetjee Jeejeebhoy, July 12, 1845; Box Manifests,
1853; PLB, A.M., to J.J., Sept. 19, 1843; UC, India,
Aug. 15, 1844. Also Ledgers, 1844; Ledgers, 1846-1847.

57. See Fairbank, Trade and Diplomacy, Chap. 21 "Wu Chien-
     chang and the 'Cantonization" of Shanghai 1852-1853,"
     pp. 393-409. One Cantonese merchant, among the large
     numbers who moved north just before or with foreign
     merchants, was credited with the rapid development of
     trade at Shanghai in the early forties. He and his agents
     had tapped the tea and silk districts of the Shanghai
     hinterland, channeling them to the new port, and had
     facilitated the import of manufactured goods and opium.
     Fairbank, Trade and Diplomacy, p. 220.

58. UC, Reports, 1848-1849.

59. CLB, June 4, 1844.

60. CLB, HK. to Sh., Feb. 18, 1852.   UC, Sh., to David Jardine,
     Aug. 3, 1851. See also Shanghai Accounts, 1854-1855.

61. "There has been no improvement in our imports owing to
     reported serious reverses on the side of the government
     in Honan and Hupeh. Fighting has been heavy and the
     dealers are cautious." ILB to J.J.. Jan. 9, 1853.
     "The insurgents, it is said, have recently taken the
     important Malwa market of Tientsin at the entrance of
     Pei-ho. We fear it will cut demand at Woosung as
     dealers are worried about distribution." Ibid., Sept. 4, 1853.
     UC, HK., 1858, n.d. Also several references to "Mandarin
     squeeze" in the India correspondence from Hong Kong.

62. ILB to J. Hadow, Bombay, Mar. 14, 1852.

63. "We cannot command the demand or foresee the sudden rapid
     fluctuations now characteristic of the trade." UC, H.K.,
     May 19, 1855.

64. UC, Calcutta, Dec. 4, 1853.

65. UC, Shanghai, Sh. to H.K., Oct. 22, 1856.

66. Forbes, p. 71. The pawnshops were called "three per cent
     per month shops" and were often "immensely rich." However,
     Forbes' book is dated 1848. Investment opportunities in
     China in the sixties had been limited. The Shanghai Share
     Circular listed bank stock (The Hong Kong and Shanghai
     Banking Corporation), eight insurance companies (The North
     China Insurance Company, Union Insurance Society, Yangtze
     Insurance Company, China Trader's Insurance Company,
     China and Japan Marine Insurance Company, Victoria Fire
     Insurance Company, China Fire Insurance Company), not
     including Jardine, Matheson and Company's Canton Insurance
     Society which was a private company, and three steamer
     companies (Shanghai Steam Navigation Company, Union Steam
     Navigation Company, and the North China Steamer Company).
     At that time, none of these were very attractive investments
     and capital was regularly remitted to London in tea or silk
     or to India in gold and silver, for investment in opium
     or Indian government securities. See Box, Printed
     Materials, 1864.

67. IMC, Reports on Trade at the Treaty Ports (Shanghai,
     1866, 1867).

68. Opium continued important in the financing of trade. See
     North China Herald, May 1877, p. 488.

69. See Accounts, Journals and Ledgers, 1860, 1865, 1870 and 1873. See also PLB-India, 1860-1873.

70. "Lord Elgin is said to view the legalization of Opium import favourably but it is best for us not to interfere. In addressing him with reference to the Treaty we have touched upon it in general terms." PLB-India, to J.A. Baumbach, Bombay, Aug. 6, 1858. "You will note by our circular that it is definitely arranged that the article is to be legalized subject to a duty of Tls. 30 per chest. This will not come into operation until the new tariff does, which may not be for some months yet. The immediate effect should increase the demand for drug rather than otherwise, but it will no doubt also encourage the growth of native poppy. Prices in India must be looked to if we are to compete successfully here. Joseph Jardine's letter to the Earl of Elgin is in BPP, 1859, XXXIII, 83. The firm's correspondence advocated legalization and steadily expressed approval of Elgin's diplomacy. See PLB, India, 1858-1859.

71. PLB, India, to R.J. Jeejeebhoy, Bombay, May 29, 1861. Commenting on an increased duty upon Malwa, Alexander Perceval wrote that "the new tax and the high price of Bengal will doubtless stimulate cultivation of native drug and, in the end, do away with trade in foreign opium altogether."

72. ILB, to G. Brown, Calcutta, Oct. 15, 1861.

73. UC, Amoy, Sept. 13, 1861 and Ledgers, 1861.

74. PLB, India, to G. Brown, Feb. 21, 1862 and several other references to investment on the firm's account in the same volume. See Ledgers and Journals, 1860-1865. This figure represents the total of opium accounts.

75. A. Wright, ed. Twentieth Century Impressions of Hong Kong, Shanghai, and other Treaty Ports of China (London, 1908), p. 224. See also North China Herald (April 1880), p. 416.

76. UC, Bombay, Aug. 24, 1855.

77. UC, Manifests, 1833-1834, ship Omega, consignment of Opium from D. Sassoon, Bombay.

78. A. Wright, p. 224. David Sassoon owned opium clippers but, in the 1850's they were not referred to by Jardine, Matheson and Company captains.

79. PLB, India to C.B. Skinner, Calcutta, Mar. 4, 1855; ibid., G.M. Robertson, Aug. 15, 1858.

80. "There is a steady increase in Opium deliveries. I cannot
    impress upon you too strongly the vast importance of care-
    fully watching the proceedings of [the Sassoons] and
    speculators whose activities are seriously upsetting prices
    here." PLB-India to G. Brown, Calcutta, July 19, 1862.

81. PLB, India to F.F. Lidderdale, Bombay, July 14, 1871 and
    UC, Bombay from J. Jeejeebhoy, May 21, 1854.

82. The growing superiority of Sassoon's puzzled Jardine for
    several years: "Your opium advices are again unaccountable
    and I am surprised that shippers are found at prices which
    cannot but lose money. The state of the China market appears
    to be ignored and it will be curious to watch how long this
    ruinous business can be carried on. Any permanent improve-
    ment can only be brought about by limited shipments from
    your side." PLB, India, to F.F. Lidderdale, Bombay,
    Aug. 17, 1868.

83. Correspondence in the autumn of 1870 followed a rising curve
    of desperation: "[Oct. 1870] We have charged our usual
    commission of 3 per cent in the A/Sales but you are free
    to return 1/2 per cent. In future we shall be glad to
    receive consignments at 2 per cent as some do -- or take
    1 per cent!...glad if reductions influence opium business
    to us..." PLB, India, J.R. Bullen-Smith, Calif., Oct. 16, 1870.

84. PLB, India, J.R. Bullen-Smith, Calif., Apr. 17, 1871.

85. "We are pleased that you consider your threat to enter
    into competition with them on their own terms is likely
    to curtail their monopoly practices." PLB-India to
    R. Eduljee, Bombay, May 8, 1871.

86. Ibid., Jan. 9, 1871.

87. UC, Sh. to HK., F.B. Johnson to J. Whittall, Mar. 17, 1871.

88. "The old trade of foreigners buying to supply the various
    northern markets has entirely died out and what little
    local [Hong Kong-Canton] consumption goes on is supplied
    by [Sassoons] on credit in a sort of retail way....The
    trade altogether has gone to the dogs and my surprise is
    the infatuation still shown on your side..." PLB, India,
    to Remington and Company, Bombay, Aug. 2, 1872.

89. See Accounts, Journals and Ledgers, 1850-1870 and UC,
    London, from Matheson and Company, July 18, 1868. [Sir]
    Robert Jardine referred to these estimates.

90. See Section of Accounts for an indication of the volume and
    value of the firm's opium business, 1850-1870. It is not
    possible to reach precise totals but the Matheson and Company
    opium account, for instance, 1863-1864, had Tls. 7,235,590
    to its credit when the gross business of the firm totaled
    Tls. 12,237,395.

II. The Cotton Trade

1. H.D. Fong, "Cotton Industry and Trade in China," The Chinese
   Social-Political Science Review, 16:392 (1932-1933).

2. ILB to J.J. & Co., Feb. 9, 1843; July 17, 1845; Feb. 27, 1846.

3. Ibid., Aug. 5, 1846.

4. A. Michie, The Englishman in China During the Victorian Era
   (London, 1900), I, 173.

5. "We are sending cotton staple to the north. There is no
   demand here (Hong Kong - Canton) but demand is reported
   at Amoy (Feb. 1843)... Raw cotton is very dull (March 1844)
   ... Nothing doing in cotton. Jeejeebhoy and Company advise
   that 1400 are being sent forward with other shipments to
   follow, and the article is as usual unmovable. (April 1844)."
   In the final months of 1844 it was noted with great relief
   that the consignments of 1843 had finally been moved off the
   firm's books; throughout 1844 even reports of a poor
   Nanking crop did not improve demand at Canton. Chinese
   merchants told Jardine's compradore, or linguist, that
   poor crops had affected interprovincial trade and had
   repressed demand for 'nankeens' [Chinese piece goods]
   in many areas. "It will be impossible to get cash for
   cotton this year [1845] and we shall have to load, bye and
   bye, about 4000 tons of tea. We must realize on $700,000
   of Jeejeebhoy cotton." CLB, HK. to coast, Feb. 5, 1843,
   Mar. 11, 1844, Apr. 5, 1844; UC,, HK-local, Nov. 19, 1844;
   CLB, HK. to A.G. Dallas, Sept. 15, 1845.

6. ILB to J.J. & Co., May 24, 1848, Aug. 14, 1850. See also
   Ledgers, 1848-1852, on J/A cotton shipments.

7. ILB to J.J. & Co., July 5, 1854. David Jardine wrote
   that "we are forwarding to Amoy whole shiploads of cotton
   ..." Also, UC, Amoy, Sept. 17, 1854.

8. CLB, HK.-Sh., Sept. 8, 1852.

9. UC, Shanghai, A.G. Dallas, July 1, 1853.

10. ILB, to J.J. & Co., Jan. 2, 1856. The firm urged Jeejeebhoy
to limit the entire annual export from Bombay to 120,000
bales per annum.

11. UC, Sh., from J. Whittall, July 4, 1863.

12. UC, HK. from M. & Co., Sept. 5, 1864.

13. Accounts, Ewo Bank, Shanghai, 1863-1864.

14. PLB, India to F.F. Lidderdale, Aug. 10, 1868.

15. PLB, India to E.W. Fogo, Bombay, Aug. 17, 1872.

16. Yang Tuan-liu and H.B. Han, Statistics of China's Foreign
Trade During the Last Sixty-Five Years (Nanking, 1931),
p. 18. Table 5 gives the value of import trade by classes
of commodities. The 1871 level was not reached again
before 1900.

17. Explanations included: (1) that the Chinese did not favor
the foreign cloth; (2) that they were themselves a manufacturing people; and (3) that the exactions of Chinese
customs houses inflated prices. Each of these points was
refuted: (1) An effort must be made to meet Chinese needs
and tastes; (2) China is not a manufacturing country in the
Western sense, and (3) the belief prevalent in Hong Kong
that China customs tax British goods until they are no
longer competitive is incorrect. The true reasons,
according to G.W. Cooke the Times correspondent, were that
Britain had been beaten by fair competition in the China
market, that British failure could be attributed to
ignorance of Chinese needs, that British merchants in
China did not favor British exports, and, finally, that
China was still largely "unopened." Jardine's experience
as piece goods importers throws light upon this analysis
of the trade between the wars and justifies his criticism
of larger manufacturing firms. G.W. Cooke, China (London:
Routledge and Company, 1858), pp. 185-209.

18. Cooke, p. 199.

19. ELB, HK. to Europe, Apr. 25, 1848 and UC, HK.-local, Market
Report, June, 1850.

20. PLB. A.M. to James Abel-Smith, Aug. 10, 1843.

21. Correspondence with British exporters had begun to warn of
     a possible reaction early in 1845: "There is a poor market,
     when sales are made it is almost impossible to realize for
     cash." UC, Sh.-HK., Apr. 3, 1845.

22. UC, Sh.-HK., Nov. 27, 1845.

23. ELB, to M. & Co., Sept. 5, 1848, and Sept. 14, 1848.

24. BPP, Correspondence relating to the Earl of Elgin's special
     mission to China and Japan, 1857-1859, 1859, XXXIII,
     243-251. Report of W.H. Mitchell to Sir George Bonham.

25. N.A. Pelcovitz, Old China Hands and the Foreign Office
     (New York, 1948), p. 17, summarizing Mitchell.

26. UC, Canton Local, Sept. 5, 1850. Acum, their Shanghai
     compradore, believed that manufactured goods would sell
     in large volume when the rebellion had ended and prosperity
     had returned to devastated districts. UC, Sh.-HK.,
     July 21, 1857.

27. Box, Sh. Accounts, 1857, 1858.

28. Silver, as a trade commodity, was much more important in
     the profit and loss accounts because of commissions earned
     on Exchange, a function performed by the firm through
     Matheson and Company in the absence of a developed banking
     system; shipping and insurance accounts also profited from
     bullion movement. The firm's vessels carried silver
     bullion from China to India each month, remitting profit
     on opium sales to Indian houses or their own funds for
     investment in future shipments. When silver became an
     import, their tea vessels began to bring valuable cargoes
     from Europe and India to pay for the increasing export of
     tea and silk, while opium clippers and steamers continued
     to carry treasure back to India. Shipments of great value
     were not uncommon in the fifties, when volume of opium
     sales doubled and prices held firm, although Jardine's
     apparently retained the bulk of their own profit in China
     for use there or for remission to London in tea or silk.
     See ILB and E.K. Bks.

29. Other legal imports, woolens and metals (iron, lead, steel,
     tin plates) were minor items regularly included in Jardine,
     Matheson and Company monthly circulars. None approached
     large volumes and there were fewer woolen goods sold in
     the fifties than there had been in the thirties. The
     firm had begun in 1845 to carry rice from Southeast Asia

and miscellaneous goods from the straits, selling most of
the former at Canton and the latter at Hong Kong or
Shanghai. Though it benefited the firm's shipping account
and yielded satisfactory profit, there was no hope for
much development of this trade channel as China needed
"grain" in emergencies only, straits produce not at all.
ELB, David Jardine to S. Mendel, Manchester, Mar. 6, 1855.
UC, London, from Hayter and Howell's, London, Jan. 9, 1854.

30. ELB, to S. Mendel, Manchester, Sept. 6, 1869.

31. CLB, to Elles and Company, Amoy, Aug. 16, 1868.

32. IMC, Reports on Trade at the Treaty Ports, Tientsin, 1866
    (Shanghai, 1867).

33. See Accounts, Ledgers and Journals, 1867-1873.

34. UC, Sh.-HK., to J.M. & Co., Nov. 18, 1872.

35. Ibid.

36. UC, Sh.-Hankow, to J.M. & Co. See also Commercial Reports,
    China, No. 2 (1883), Shanghai; "The poverty of the masses,
    no doubt, has a great deal to do with it, but it is well
    known that our manufactures are greatly appreciated in
    China by those that can afford to buy them and it is
    certain that the consumption would be greatly increased
    if they could be laid down at inland markets at more
    reasonable rates." p. 135. Also UC, Great Britain,
    Oct. 19, 1880 and Nov. 6, 1880. No statistics given.

37. UC, Shanghai, J. Bell-Irving to E. Cunningham, Russell
    and Company, Aug. 17, 1878.

38. PLB, Sh.-HK., to W. Keswick, Jan. 17, 1879 and PCLB,
    Sh-HK. to W. Keswick, Dec. 20, 1878.

39. Commercial Reports, China, No. 1 (1880) Shanghai, p. 29.

40. Ibid., p. 30.

41. Ibid., p. 36.

42. Ibid.

43. Ibid. The consul had heard that shares in the Chinese
    Company were not being taken by Chinese merchants because
    they "are possibly afraid of the official connection with
    the scheme." The China Merchants Steam Navigation Company
    was said to be a warning. The China Overland Trade Report,
    Hong Kong, Mar. 1, 1879, commented on the danger of official
    control of the mill and cited the China Merchants Steam
    Navigation Company as an example of destructive official

interference. The paper was angered by Li's statement
in his correspondence with Peng that "the foreign hongs in
Shanghai excel in powers of cheating, one and all, they
swindle you first and go to law with you afterwards."

44. Ibid. Cheng was a former compradore of Butterfield & Swire
and in 1880 an associate manager of the China Merchants
Steam Navigation Company.

45. "Our best information holds that China cotton cannot be
spun into yarn which will make grey shirtings, and that
the highest count of yarn into which it can be spun is
No. 20." UC, HK., from J. Bell-Irving, Feb. 4, 1879.

46. PCLB, HK., G.B., to Platt Bros. & Co., Oldham, Nov. 14, 1878.

47. PLB, Sh.-HK., to W. Keswick, May 5, 1879.

48. See The China Review, Hong Kong, 10:5 (July 1881 - June 1892).
The writer also mentions Tso Tsung-tang's "woolen factory"
at Lanchow, Kansu, operating with the help of 13 Germans.
"...as soon as the Chinese become accustomed to employ
machinery we fail to see why (they)...should not succeed
in weaving as well as Europeans and at much less cost."
But the enterprise failed soon after Tso's death.

49. PCLB, Sh.-HK., to W. Keswick, Nov. 19, 1879.

50. Ibid., Mar. 12, 1880. A year earlier W. Keswick had
written that "the Chinese use Bombay yarn (a losing trade)
for the manufacture of coarse cloths such as are generally
used throughout the country. The yarn being cheaper than
the people themselves spin from their own primitive machines
and this for the past two years." UC:Pr, HK., 1854-1882.

51. H.B. Morse, The International Relations of the Chinese
Empire (London, 1910-1918), II, 316-317.

52. PLB, Sh.-HK., to W. Keswick, Dec. 29, 1882.

53. Ibid.

54. Ibid., Jan. 3, 1883.

55. UC, HK.-Sh. to W. Paterson. Jan. 20, 1883. See Holcombe, p. 21,
for a summary of "Prince Kung's" (Ch'un) arguments against mach

56. UC, HK.-Sh., to W. Paterson, Jan. 25, 1883.

57. Ibid., Jan. 3, 1883.

58. PLB, Sh.-HK., to J. Macgregor, July 22, 1889. Also: North
China Herald: Aug. 13, 1888, Aug. 15, 1888, Mar. 17, 1893,
on cotton mill plans.

59. PLB Sh.-HK., to J. Keswick (J. Macgregor died in November 1893), June 1, 1894.

60. "On the front page will be found the prospectus of the first cotton mill in China started by foreigners and under foreign control; for though the promoters thought it well to put two Chinese on the provisional committee, the control of the mill will be entirely in foreign hands. It is appropriate that Messrs. J.M. & Co., who have fought for the machinery question so long, should be first in the field with a foreign mill. The eager demand for the share in the enterprise is shown by the fact that only 2,000 shares of the 7,500 to be first issued remained to be allotted on the 1st instant, and we cannot doubt that in the able hands of such a leading firm in China the Ewo Cotton Spinning & Weaving Co. will be a conspicuous success." China Mail (July 8, 1895), "Ewo Cotton Spinning & Weaving Co.," North China Daily News. By 1908, the shareholders, most of whom were Chinese, had received in dividends Tls. 28 per each 100-tael share.

III. Years of Transition and Trade

1. Quoted in K.C. Liu, Anglo-American Steamship Rivalry in China 1862-1874, (Cambridge, Mass., 1962), p. 139. This study is basic to an understanding of shipping enterprise during the "years of transition."

2. UC, Sh.-HK., to J. Whittall, July 21, 1872.

3. See CLB, February - March 1861. J.M. & Co. agents were established at Tamsui (Taiwan), Tientsin, Newchwang and Swatow in 1861, at Hankow one year later. Their steamers began to call at Tientsin and Newchwang in 1861.

4. ILB:Pr, G. Brown, Calcutta, Dec. 18, 1860.

5. UC:L, Sh., Sept. 6, 1865.

6. IMC, Reports on Trade at the Treaty Ports, 1865, Newchwang (Shanghai, 1866). Most of the "foreign trade" of Newchwang consisted of imports transshipped at Shanghai of Yangtze produce carried north in foreign ships and "Newchwang junks."

7. Ibid., Tientsin, p. 25.

8. Ibid., Hankow, p. 41.

9. Ibid., Amoy, p. 65.

10. Ibid., Shanghai, pp. 77-91.

11. UC, Sh.-HK., Dec. 4, 1848.

12. CLB, HK.-Sh., Aug. 6, 1852.

13. UC, Foochow, Oct. 16, 1854.

14. ILB, to R.W. Crawford, Bombay, July 3, 1856 and ILB,
    to J.J., Sept. 4, 1856.

15. IMC, Reports on Trade at the Treaty Ports, 1866, Shanghai,
    (Shanghai, 1967), pp. 1-17.

16. Ibid., p. 14. One hundred and sixteen of these banks were
    said to exist in Shanghai in 1866.

17. IMC, Reports on Trade at the Treaty Ports, 1867, Canton,
    pp. 57-62.

18. IMC, Reports on Trade at the Treaty Ports, 1866, Foochow,
    pp. 21-32. Ibid., Tientsin, pp. 83-104.

19. W.F. Mayers, N.B. Dennys and St. Charles King, eds., Treaty
    Ports of China and Japan (London and Hong Kong, 1867), p. 18.
    At Canton "no less than elsewhere in China the native
    dealers are rapidly absorbing in their own hands the dealings
    which until lately were the means of enriching European
    houses of business..." p. 200. Chinese businessmen became
    of great interest to the European and American Treaty Port
    communities in the sixties, but contact was difficult.
    "As is well known what are ordinarily considered as the
    Chinese merchants are only the factotums of the real traders,
    who keep in the background, and for reasons of commercial
    policy who carefully avoid direct contact with the outer
    barbarism. It is very much more difficult than is
    ordinarily thought, even for men speaking the language to
    come much into social contact with respectable trading
    Chinese classes; and it may be many years yet before we
    get farther than the half educated pidgin English speaking
    individuals, who have hitherto represented the Chinese
    traders with Europeans." Supreme Court and Consular
    Gazette and Law Reporter, for H.B.M. Supreme Court and
    Provincial Courts and the Consular Courts of China and Japan,
    Shanghai, 1867-1869, Oct. 10, 1868.

20. W.F. Mayers, N.B. Dennys and St. Charles King, eds.,
    pp. 19, 365.

21. IMC, Reports on Trade at the Treaty Ports, 1869,
    Hankow, p. 37.

22. See especially Commercial Reports of Her Majesty's Consuls
    in China, China, No. 2, 1872, Shanghai.

23. UC, Sh.-HK., to J. Whittall, May 29, 1871. The aim was to
    enlist Chinese support for a new shipping company.

24. IMC, Reports, 1869. Suggestions for the revision of the
    Chinese Customs and Tariff Regulations, p. 19.

25. "The availability of foreign vessels has always been regarded
    as an immense boon by the native merchants on the coast,
    and has also been favourably regarded by the Officers of
    the Chinese Government." Ibid.

26. IMC, Reports on Trade at the Treaty Ports, 1872,
    Tientsin, p. 46.

27. See Commercial Reports, 1870-1885, especially China, No. 2
    (1870), the report of Michie and Francis, Hankow, 1869-1870.
    Experience at Hankow, Kukiang, etc. showed that the
    Chinese would take over native trade and part of the
    foreign trade but Chinese "are frequently assisted by
    foreign capital, loans on the security of goods, and
    advances on coast and river shipments." Also, China,
    No. 2 (1872), Shanghai, which estimates that 50 per cent
    of the shares in the Shanghai Steam Navigation Company are
    held by Chinese.

28. Commercial Reports, China, No. 1 (1875), Chinkiang, p. 205.

29. Commercial Reports, China, No. 6 (1874), Newchwang.

30. Commercial Reports, China, No. 1 (1877), Shanghai, p. 33.

31. Commercial Reports, China, No. 3 (1876), Hankow, p. 46.
    The consul wrote that the Chinese looked upon foreign
    appliances as a means of extending their wealth; they had
    invested in steamship companies, banks, insurance companies,
    and mining companies.

32. Ellsworth Carlson, The Kaiping Mines, 1877-1912 (Cambridge,
    Mass., 1957), p. 3.

33. Teng Ssu-yü and John K. Fairbank, China's Response to the
    West: A Documentary Survey, 1839-1923 (Cambridge, Mass.,
    1954), p. 109.

34. Ibid., p. 110.

IV. Cooperation with the Bureaucracy

1. On the depreciation of silver, see Yang Tuan-lin and
    H.B. Han, Statistics of China's Foreign Trade During
    the Last Sixty-Five Years (Nanking, 1951). For background
    data, 1885-1894, see Morse, International Relations,
    II, 390-415.

2. An editorial in the China Mail (Apr. 19, 1875) referred to
    a memorial of Li Hung-chang's to the Empress Regent which
    urged that foreign learning and sciences be placed on a
    par with the standard subjects in the literary examinations
    of the empire: "We look upon the action as of more
    importance than the opening of mines or the building
    of railways. Li will assuredly carve for himself a niche
    in the temple of fame second only to that occupied
    by Confucius."

3. Teng and Fairbank, p. 133, for a brief reference to this
    decade: "One has the impression that this was a period
    when the old order was able to coast along, in the
    benevolent shadow of Victorian Britain." and p. 164 et seq.
    See also J.H. Wilson, China: Travels and Investigations
    in the Middle Kingdom (New York, 1888). He wrote that
    "the Chinese Government is so isolated, vague and
    inaccessible, as to render it almost impossible for
    foreigners to reach, influence, or move it, while it
    is peculiarly subject to the control of conservatism
    and prejudice..." p. 198.
        It may happen, too, that there is a great and prosperous
    enterprise, working under Government auspices, and supported
    by Government funds. It cannot be attacked, or complained
    of, or squeezed, or subjected to any of those processes
    which are so often put into execution in China against
    wealthy corporations. Why? Because of its connection
    with the Government? By no means. The true strength of
    such a corporation would lie in the fact of its connection
    with rich retired officials, or members of the Bankers' or
    the Opium Guild." North China Herald (May 1882), p. 60.

4. See A. Feuerwerker, China's Early Industrialization
    (Cambridge, Mass., 1958), pp. 242-244.

5. During these years "normal" agency business, Import and
    Export, continued to command a large share of managerial
    attention though investment in the servicing of trade had
    grown apace since 1870; the value of Jardine's shares
    in joint-stock enterprises managed by the firm and in the
    Hong Kong and Shanghai Bank (1000 shares of par value
    $125) in April 1885, was:

	Taels
Hunt's Wharf Property	213,846
Jardine Piers and Godowns	331,000
Canton Insurance Office	36,000
Hong Kong Fire Insurance Company	44,100
Hong Kong and Whampoa Dock Company	81,568
Hong Kong, Canton and Macao SS Company	39,672
Shanghai and Hongkew Wharves	30,962
Indo-China Steam Navigation Company	817,560
Hong Kong and Shanghai Bank	463,968
China Sugar Refining	109,858
Luzon Sugar Refining	119,850

See Journals and Ledgers, Hong Kong, April, 1885.
     Three major functions, banking, shipping and insurance
dominated the investment market which reflected the non-
productive commercial character of the Treaty Port system.
Jardine's had taken advantage of the opportunities available
in these fields ancillary to trade, although the amount of
capital annually available to the firm for re-investment in
China is not known. They wished to multiply investment
opportunities, particularly those related to railroad construction and mining, which would stimulate commission
business conducted by agencies mediating between the Chinese
on the one hand and Western capital, manufacturers and
technical skills on the other and provide new uses for
profits made in China. See also China Mail, Mar. 25, 1884.
"...J.M. & Co., whose commissions alone, report says, are
equal to perhaps £150,000 a year." Ibid., July 8, 1884
article "Railways in China": "Now there is no doubt abun-
dance of foreign capital ready to be employed, the owners
of which would be only too glad to lend it to China for
this purpose." Rates mentioned: 8 per cent, 7 per cent,
or even 6 per cent. An indication of Jardine's financial
strength and ability to act as government agents may be
found in the 1885 Accounts as well as in the record of
the firm's experience and range. Assets totaled over

eight million taels (Tls. 8,000,000), including more than
four million in the name of Sir Robert Jardine (W. Keswick,
Tls. 594,788; F.B. Johnson, Tls. 408,833; Wm. Paterson,
Tls. 189,429; J.J. Keswick, Tls. 171,698, etc.). It is
not possible to judge how much of this total represented
profits available for reinvestment nor exactly what
percentage of total assets listed represented previous
investment in the Treaty Ports. But a rough calculation
would indicate that more than half of the firm's total
capital was invested in steamships, Treaty Port real estate,
banking, insurance and produce business. The range of its
business, and this substantial capital, placed its members
most favorably in their campaign to serve as catalysts in
China's commercial and industrial development.

6. J. Matheson, Present Position and Prospects of British
    Trade with China (London, 1836), p. 7.

7. See Ho Ping-ti, Studies on the Populations of China, 1368-
    1953 (Cambridge, Mass., 1959), p. 238, on the effects of
    the Taiping rebellion.

8. The loan was guaranteed by Bonds of the Chinese Customs at
    Canton; a continuation of pre-Treaty practices whereby
    Cantonese officials acquired access to the profits of
    foreign trade through Chinese associated with foreign firms.
    UC, Canton-local, J.M. & Co., May 10, 1858.

9. UC, HK. to A. Perceval, Nov. 15, 1864 and Apr. 6, 1865.
    See Accounts, Journals, Hong Kong, 1868-1869 in which
    Tls. 1,501,360 is credited to the Opium Account in July 1868;
    the Journals, HK., May 1874, credit Tls. 202,073 to the
    Opium Account. Both figures represent current investment.

10. Robert Hart's aim in these early foreign loans was to
    bolster the financial power of the central government
    as opposed to provincial authorities, whose power had
    become largely autonomous during and after the Taiping
    Rebellion; Hart seems to have believed that a strong
    central government, if controlled by officials moderately
    sympathetic to reform and backed by Maritime Customs
    Revenue, would be the best hope of national regeneration.
    Such a government could be "placed" in the international
    money markets, and funds could be secured at reasonable
    interest to initiate the projects, military and industrial,
    which would allow China to break out of her cycle of
    economic and administrative decline. Hart's efforts to
    strengthen the central government have also been described

by Hu Sheng, Imperialism and Chinese Politics (Peking, 1955) as fastening the fetters of "financial capital" round the necks of the Chinese, but his conduct through years of such negotiations, and his attitude to large Western firms who were normally without thought for any purpose beyond profit, immediate and future, refutes the charge "that he devised and put into effect the whole system of foreign imperialist control over the customs revenue administration of China." See S.F. Wright, Hart and the Chinese Customs (Belfast, 1950), pp. 365-366 and passim.

11. UC, Sh.-local, to J. Whittall, May 19, 1867.

12. Ibid., Nov. 29, 1867.

13. Accounts, Journals, and Ledgers, Sh. 1875 and UC, Sh.-HK., to W. Keswick. Also Morse, Vol. III, Appendix A; Rate of interest to public given as 8 per cent and dates of repayment 1876-1885. (The firm did not act as ultimate lender and the loan was not publicly issued; it was "privately placed in Shanghai." On April 6, 1875, only one-half the loan was subscribed but, using its own and borrowed funds, the firm delivered one million taels on that date. They managed to dispose of the whole issue within the next seventy days and repayment began as scheduled, i.e. £57,000 in September, 1875, and at each due date thereafter until the debt had been cleared.) UC, HK. to J. Whittall, Sept. 16, 1875.

14. "Evidently Matheson and Co. don't wish to have anything to do with the proposed loan..." PLB, Sh. to HK., to W. Keswick, Sept. 23, 1876.

15. See Yang Tuan-Liu and H.B. Han, Table IV, p. 10. Tls. 31,401,935 worth of silk was exported in 1876.

16. PLB, Sh.-HK. to W. Keswick, Mar. 8, 1877.

17. ILB-P., HK.-Calcutta, to J.R. Bullen-Smith, June 16, 1877. The London and San Francisco offices of the Bank shipped altogether £850,000 bar silver and the Hong Kong office supplied the rest. The Loan was issued in China at 8 per cent and 98. The records of the Bank do not agree with the firm's account as they show that J.M. & Co. received $50,000 for help in negotiations but the loan was not a "joint-venture." (J.R. Jones: private letter, Sept. 12, 1962).

18. PLB, Sh.-HK., to W. Keswick, July 20, 1878. "It appears there is a hitch about the Edict for the loan." According to the China Mail (HK., May 13, 1878), the loan was for

Tls. 3,500,000, Tls. 1,500,000 lent by the Hong Kong and
Shanghai Bank, the balance "being subscribed chiefly by
Chinese at Shanghai and Ningpo."

19. PLB, Sh.-HK., to W. Keswick, July 5, 1879, referring to
credit balance (Tls. 50,000) of the C.C.S.N. on June 23, 1879.

20. PLB, Sh.-HK., to W. Keswick, Oct. 14, 1879.

21. Ibid., and UC, HK to J. Bell-Irving, Oct. 21, 1879.

22. PLB, Sh.-HK., to W. Keswick, Feb. 10, 1881. In 1885 the
North China Herald commented: "At the present time the
whole public debt of China amounts only to Taels 2,740,000
and $2,789,400.25 or about £1,160,000. The instalments
and interest on the loans have always been duly met, and
so small were the amounts originally borrowed, considering
the extent and resources of the country, that if anything
like a reasonable system of finance existed in the Empire
there would never have been any necessity to apply for money
to the foreigner. But the semi-independence of the provinces,
and the reckless way in which money was squandered on arsenals
and useless vessels-of-war, coming upon the customary
corruption and maladministration, had reduced many of
the Viceroys to official destitution." North China Herald
(Jan. 14, 1885).

23. UC, HK.-Sh., to J.J. Keswick, Feb. 3, 1881. William
Keswick, then head of the firm, wrote: "Morrison has
gone to Tientsin to see Li, and he must have exact
information of loan conditions. Can we float a loan
through our London friends? There is talk of a Tientsin-
Peking Railway which would mean a loan of £1,000,000."
During the eighties Morrison was frequently in Peking,
explaining his proposals to members of the Tsungli Yamen
or to any official willing to consider them. In the
event of a successful contract, Jardine's would handle
orders for material, take charge of accounts, and divide
commission with him. His chief task was to prepare
specifications of materials to be ordered for proposed
railways: (UC, HK.-Sh., to J. Keswick, July 11, 1885).
"It will be to Morrison's advantage..to have contracts,
if any such are obtainable, made through us and through
our Native Agency now opened up by Mr. Mandl...I should
like to see the intention of the Chinese to construct
railways so far advanced as to be only a question between
Morrison and ourselves what our position should be. I fear
graver causes for delay exist than such a question!"
Morrison toured China "covering 2000 miles on foot and
in other ways" during the late seventies. See his article

on railway construction and the "new China Party" (i.e. "self-strengthening" officials) in China Mail, Feb. 11, 1879. He wrote: "...there is no undeveloped country in the world where railways are more needed, or where they could prove more remunerative than here."

24. PLB, Sh.-HK., to W. Keswick (Copy of letter to James Morrison), Feb. 3, 1881.

25. PLB, Sh.-HK., to F.B. Johnson, June 12, 1881. "During the past 12 months China has had a rude waking up. An army of defence had to be collected at short notice to repel an enemy [Russia] who was at the gate of China. At every step her efforts were paralyzed by the want of...railways and the telegraph. To the advantage of these the statesmen of China had for years been keenly alive but in deference to the old leaders of the Palace and their advisers the dolts of the Academy they had tried to do without them...Were China to consent to give requisite guarantees to English-men regarding construction and management, capital in plenty would be forthcoming for railways here; without such guarantees the purses of Lombard Street will not be opened." (The Times correspondent, Shanghai, Apr. 16, 1881, quoted in the China Mail).

26. Ibid. The firm was wary of Detring, fearing that he might favor his German countrymen although he had made gestures of goodwill toward Jardine's; in the autumn of 1880, when there was a rumor of war between China and Russia, he asked the firm if they would be willing to have the China Merchants' fleet transferred to their name. PLB, Sh.-HK. to W. Keswick, Oct. 11, 1886.

27. PLB, Sh.-HK., to F.B. Johnson, June 12, 1881.

28. Ibid., July 4, 1881 and Hummel, II, p. 767.

29. PLB, Sh.-HK., to F.B. Johnson, July 15, 1881 and Aug. 15, 1881.

30. UC, Sh.-HK., from J. Morrison, Aug. 13, 1881.

31. PLB, Sh.-HK., to F.B. Johnson, July 18, 1881.

32. Ibid., Aug. 8, 1881.

33. Ibid., Aug. 15, 1881.

34. Ibid., Aug. 23, 1881. The firm depended upon Matheson and Company to support most of its loan proposals and if this support was withheld, large or joint-stock investment schemes could not be pursued. In this case, Matheson and Company urged caution because the loan was, plainly, to be

made to "a mere provincial authority" (removable at any
moment by an Edict from Peking) and there seemed to be
an element of great risk unless such guarantees as Li might
give for eventual repayment would be honored by his
successor. Their basic position was that any proposal
brought before the public in London would have to be for
a loan formally authorized by imperial edict, announced
in the Peking Gazette, certified by the British legation
and if the Foreign (Maritime) Customs were made special
security for any loan this must be acknowledged by the
inspector general. Jardine's expected the solicitation
of large loans for "public works" and it was these which
Mathesons had in mind when discussing safeguards. A
recent Hong Kong and Shanghai Bank loan to provincial
authorities had drawn their disapproval. Matheson and
Company very much wanted business of this nature, yet
their insistence that the first trial should be within
the security of imperial guarantee and official support
indicated a strong distrust of provincial authority and
disbelief in the treaty port estimate of Li Hung-chang as
de facto ruler of China; the imperial seal was regarded
as the most certain security. UC, London, M. & Co.,
to J.M. & Co., Nov. 11, 1881.

35. Ibid., Sept. 10, 1881.

36. UC, HK.-Sh., to J. Keswick, Oct. 16, 1881.

37. UC, R. Jardine to W. Paterson, Sh., May 29, 1883.

38. UC, HK.-Sh., to J. Keswick, Sept. 10, 1881.

39. Ibid., Sept. 15, 1881.

40. Jardine's correspondence does not specify the conditions.

41. Ibid., Sept. 15, 1881.

42. Wilson, p. 91.

43. When the Fournier Convention had been signed and the war
     apparently ended, J. Keswick wrote: "The opening of
     Kwangtung, Kwangse, and Yunnan are reported as secured by
     the French Treaty of Peace with China and the settlement of
     the Tonquin difficulty by this concession and by the
     recognition of a French protectorate over Tonquin and
     Annam is a most satisfactory and liberal arrangement and
     one calculated to disarm all hostile criticism of France
     as by her proceedings the condition of large populations
     will be vastly ameliorated." PLB, Sh.-HK., to W. Keswick,
     Sept. 14, 1884.

44. UC, London, F.B. Johnson to W. Keswick, Sept. 26, 1884.

45. Ibid.

46. Ibid.

47. Ibid., Oct. 3, 1884. Later, W. Keswick said of the war:
    "...nothing...during the last quarter century has done more
    to make China a nation, to produce patriotic feeling,
    to bring into harmony the idea of the West and China in
    the way of progress." China Mail, Mar. 18, 1886.

48. See E.V.G. Kiernan, British Diplomacy in China, 1880-1885
    (Cambridge, England, 1939), p. 272.

49. UC, HK.-Sh., to J.M. and Company, 1884-1885. Most references
    are brief and isolated.

50. Jardine Matheson and Company had some Tls. 450,000 worth of
    the Bank's stock. See Section of Accounts, HK., 1885.

51. Jardine's also competed with the bank in many ways, as, for
    example, by providing simple banking services to officials;
    in 1884 Li Hung-chang asked the firm to provide money for
    officials of the imperial government in Formosa during the
    French blockade. This was done by their agent at Tamsui
    who paid $130,000 from December 1884 through March 1885
    to the taotai at Tamsui and to H.E. Commissioner Liu Ming-
    ch'uan, the latter an official of whom Jardine's expected
    "progressive action." Vouchers for these payments were
    sent to Li Hung-chang and repayment made at Tientsin.
    However, Li was not so easily cajoled as, soon after,
    Jardine's complained to Mackenzie Brothers and Company
    of Glasgow that they were unable to interest the viceroy
    in the purchase of "rifle factories" despite their cordial
    relations and "the many services rendered to the Viceroy
    recently." UC, Coast-Sh., Apr. 13, 1885 to J.M. and Company.

52. Ibid., Apr. 26, 1884.

53. UC, Sh.-HK., to W. Keswick, July 6, 1884.

54. UC, Peking-Tientsin, to H. Mandl, Feb. 18, 1885.

55. UC, HK.-Sh., to W. Paterson, June 17, 1885. Apparently
    Baring Brothers provided Matheson and Company with the
    full amount. Details are few in the J.M. archive; one
    volume, PLB, Sh.-HK., 1884-1885 seems to be missing.
    After negotiating the loan the firm complained that the
    British legation had not put pressure on the Tsungli
    Yamen to have the Chinese Minister in London (Tseng
    Chi-tse) sign the bonds issued there, though this was
    done in the end.

56. UC, HK.-Sh., to W. Paterson, Apr. 24, 1885.

57. Ibid., Aug. 27, 1885.

58. Ibid., Sept. 9, 1885.

V. The Firm as Special Agent to the Chinese Government

1. UC, Sh.-from Tientsin, to J. Keswick, Oct. 25, 1885.

2. Ibid., (press copy) Oct. 25, 1885. Keswick also discussed
    the founding of a Chinese language newspaper in Tientsin:
    "Detring is anxious that Dunn should bring...the necessary
    equipment to begin at once a daily issue of a Chinese
    newspaper...The impression is that with a clever and
    vigorous native organ we may succeed in driving reform
    into China and overcoming in Peking the opposition with
    which some of the Viceroy's (Li Hung-chang) patriotic
    schemes were received." Shih-pao was published by the
    Chinese Times (Tientsin, 1886-1891).

3. Ibid.

4. Ibid., Nov. 13, 1885. J.M. & Co. would form a new company,
    "The North China Engineering Co., Ltd.," to receive official
    sanction for building the line.

5. Ibid., Nov. 13, 1885 and Nov. 17, 1885.

6. Ibid., Nov. 17, 1885.

7. In one letter, Keswick said: "I am by no reason certain that
    my interviews will result in anything at present for there
    is much consternation at the Yamen in consequence of an
    Imperial Decree that was issued yesterday in Peking degrading
    Li Feng-pow (Li Feng-pao) the late minister at Berlin and
    around whom the Viceroy had striven to throw as much personal
    protection as he could influence. I understand the terms of
    the decree are severe and indicate that the ex-Minister is
    hopelessly degraded. He doubtless readily deserves his fate,
    but it nevertheless means to Li Hung-chang a defeat and will
    probably have the effect of making him less bold in carrying
    out the measures of progress he intended giving his sanction
    and protection. Ibid., Nov. 24, 1885.

8. UC, Sh.-local, Apr. 16, 1886.

9. PLB, Sh.-Tientsin, H.F. to John Dudgeon, Peking, May 21, 1887.

10. Ibid.

11. Ibid., May 23, 1887.

12. Ibid.

13. Ibid., May 27, 1887.

14. Ibid., to A. Michie, July 28, 1887.

15. PLB, Sh.-HK., to W. Keswick, Jan. 31, 1886.

16. UC, HK., 1886-1905, to J. Keswick, Sh., Jan. 16, 1886 and Feb. 6, 1886. "The intrigues at Peking have evidently been of the most evil character."

17. "The state of matters here is that Yuan has made a number of absolutely puerile corrections in the contract which the Taotai here has supported adding something more on his own account to show he is not to be outdone in zeal for the Ta-tsing dynasty. Some of them I disposed of -- others are so obviously vague that it is difficult to object and so the contract has been drawn up in English-Chinese two days ago but not a word of its being signed or even sent to Port Arthur. One clause says that before purchasing the prices are to be sent to the Chinese Minister and Yuan Taotai and if either of them think they can do better they are to telegraph Jardine Matheson and Company who are after that to guide themselves accordingly. Such a clause, if acted upon, would nullify the contract for it would force you to wait for an answer from Port Arthur and by that time the market might have gone away from you...The V.R. is in a hurry and he sent a peremptory message a week ago via Detring to Chou to say he would stand no more nonsense and he wants to hurry up the contract but he has not turned up at all, it almost looks as if Yuan and Chou were purposely delaying the thing." UC, Tientsin, to H. Mandl, Chefoo, Feb. 18, 1886.

18. Ibid., "Kao sends the enclosed to Sheng (Hsuan-huai)."

19. Ibid., Apr. 7, 1886.

20. This referred to Michie's report that the Germans had been unable to interest Gustav Detring with their railway-building proposals. Ibid., press copy, to A. Michie, Apr. 8, 1886 (replying to telegram).

21. Ibid.

22. Ibid., Apr. 22, 1886.

23. *Ibid*. An interpreter was found in Shanghai before the end
    of the month.

24. PLB, Sh-HK., to W. Keswick, July 18, 1886. "...(we) have
    long been convinced of the necessity of having Chinese
    speakers on our staff but you cannot get them ready-made
    and if you do they are costly."

25. PLB, Sh.-HK., to W. Keswick, May 1, 1886 and UC, Tientsin,
    to J. Keswick, May 19, 1886.

26. "The sooner Fliche [Jardine, Matheson's agent] comes up here
    the better so that he can play one French manufacturing
    engineer against another." UC, Tientsin, to J. Keswick,
    May 12, 1886.

27. UC, Tientsin to J. Keswick, May 19, 1886.

28. *Ibid*.

29. From the seventies Jardine's had done a large agency business
    in the sale of arms to the Chinese government; by 1885 they
    were regularly circulating drawings and price lists to their
    branches on behalf of British, French and German firms
    (Armstrong, Krupp and Creusot) which included specifications
    of rifles, machine guns, cannon, torpedo boats and submarines.
    Their agents particularly emphasized a number of suggested
    coastal defense projects (plans supplied by Messrs. Latimer,
    Clark, Muirhead and Company) after the French War. (UC,
    Formosa, D. Spence to W. Keswick, Sept. 7, 1885). Sir
    William Armstrong and Company of Newcastle were Jardine's
    principal correspondents in this business but it was never
    a smooth relationship. Very often the firm complained of
    Armstrong's slowness in sending blueprints of models and
    their reluctance to provide technical advisers in China.
    Armstrong also worked with independent agents such as J.J.
    Buchheister of Shanghai with whom Jardine's was therefore
    compelled to do business. See UC, Tientsin, 1885-1887 seriatim.

30. UC, Tientsin, to J. Keswick, July 9, 1886. "Port Arthur
    is safe, the French bowled over."

31. *Ibid*., July 29, 1886. Michie's reports indicate that
    irregular procedures including theft of contract copies
    were normal in Western efforts to secure the viceroy's
    orders: "Another sixteen page contract of (M. Thevenet's
    French Syndicate) has been in my hands and it will receive
    a rather heavy criticism at the hands of our competent man
    [Fliche] who in his interviews with the viceroy will draw
    attention to certain weak points but of course avoiding all
    pointed allusions."

32. Ibid.

33. PLB, Sh.-HK., to W. Keswick, May 16, 1886.

34. Spence's relationship with the former "soldier of fortune" was unusually affable, much to the firm's benefit, and his correspondence with the governor evokes the atmosphere of personal loyalty within the Confucian bureaucracy, where proof of personal goodwill was essential. Yet some of Spence's private remarks were decidedly unfilial: ("What a barbarian the governor of Formosa is!") Some thought that Formosa had been chosen as a place to experiment with railways and telegraphs because there would be no "Fung-Shu" [feng-shui: geomancy] problems. China Mail, Oct. 29, 1877. UC, Formosa to Liu Ming ch'uan, Nov. 18, 1886.

35. Ibid., Dec. 8, 1886.

36. PLB, Sh.-HK., to J. Bell-Irving, Nov. 7, 1886. According to J. Keswick, the bank had previously offered to lend money to Liu Ming ch'uan at 7 per cent; or at 6 1/2 per cent if for ten years.

37. "Liu, Governor of Formosa to the Ewo Hong -- Your letter has been received and noted as to the gunpowder which you have bought and stores at Hong Kong. The Gun Boat 'Fu Po' will be dispatched thither to transport it and the storage and expense will be remitted to you by Formosa (The Formosan Government)." (Sept. 16, 1889). UC, Formosa, to J.M. & Co., (Ewo).

38. PLB, Sh.-HK., to J. Bell-Irving, May 31, 1887. There are small indications of the firm's attitude toward political disorder: "You will find M. Accles' technical knowledge valuable in explaining matters to the Chinese and I hope his 'Wheelbarrow Gatling' commends itself to the Chinese mind. For clearing streets in case of riots nothing could be better." UC, Tientsin, to J. Keswick, Apr. 23, 1887.

39. PLB, Sh.-Tientsin, Hankow and Foochow, to A. Michie, Sept. 14, 1886.

40. Ibid., Aug. 15, 1886. There were reports that the French Syndicate was not only pressing for a Port Arthur contract but was also considered likely to be selected for Yellow River works: "If the Chinese in such a gigantic and important undertaking are going to throw themselves into the arms of the first man they meet there is not much use of striving for it looks as if they will go to the cheapest market irrespective of scientific value for their money."

41. UC, Tientsin, to J. Keswick, Oct. 21, 1887 and PLB, Sh-Tientsin, Hankow, Foochow, to A. Michie, Oct. 23, 1886.

42. PLB, Sh-Tientsin, Hankow, Foochow, to A. Michie, Nov. 5, 1886.

43. UC, Tientsin, to J. Keswick, Nov. 10, 1886.

44. PLB, Sh-Tientsin, Hankow, Foochow to A. Michie, Nov. 16, 1887.

45. Ibid., Dec. 21, 1887.

46. Ibid.

47. UC, Tientsin to J. Keswick, Feb. 6, 1888 and Feb. 17, 1888.

48. PLB, Sh-Tientsin, Hankow, Foochow, to A. Michie, May 14, 1888.

49. Ibid.

50. PLB, Sh.-HK., to John Macgregor, Aug. 30, 1888.

51. PLB, Sh-Tientsin, to A. Michie, Aug. 6, 1888.

52. Ibid.

53. UC, Tientsin to J. Keswick, Sept. 11, 1888. See Translation of the Peking Gazette for 1888 (Shanghai, 1889), pp. 118-119 for the decree degrading Li Ho-nien and Ch'eng-Fu which says that Tls. 9,000,000 had been spent on the project.

54. Similar proposals from the French Syndicate and a new "Manchester Syndicate" were also made; the English group offered a plan which would regulate the river from its source to its mouth for Tls. 18,000,000. PLB, Sh.-HK., to John Macgregor, Aug. 1, 1888.

VI. The Imperial Household

1. UC, Sh., to J. Keswick, Nov. 28, 1884.

2. "The Nuy-woo foo, or office of internal affairs, under an indefinite number of ta chin, or great ministers, is for the control and government of the class called 'Paou-e of the three banners' (a class of imperial slaves), and for regulating the restrictions of the palace. All affairs, civil, financial, ritual, military, penal, and operative, connected with the imperial household, are conducted under the orders of the officers of the Nuy-woo foo. These officers have likewise, in concert with the Boards

of Civil Office and of War, the appointment and regulation
of the numerous civil and military offices of subordinate
rank, connected with the imperial household. The Chinese
Repository, 4:185 (1835-1836).

3. The "Ewo Bank" had been liquidated in June 1869 shortly
after the death of the major Chinese shareholder, "Ekee."
The firm owed to his estate Tls. 283,000 in July 1869.
See Journals, Hong Kong, 1868-1869.

4. UC, Tientsin, to J. Keswick, Sept. 1, 1886. PLB, Sh.-
Tientsin, Hankow, Foochow, to A. Michie, Sept. 1, 1886.
J. Keswick wrote to a merchant who had offered his services
in Peking that "our special agent Mr. Michie has been and
still is in Peking in connection with advances to the
Imperial Household with whom he has had special financial
relations for some time..." UC, Sh.-Local, to C. Rich,
Sept. 7, 1886. Loans to the Nei-wu fu were for small
amounts, usually Tls. 200,000 each time, therefore they
did not require Matheson and Company's approval or support;
the prices of the loans varied and were figured on the
current price of money in the Treaty Ports. Payments were
usually in the form of sycee transferred by pony from
Shanghai, and occasionally Michie was embarrassed by the
firm's inability to provide a large amount requested
urgently. The firm hoped eventually to profitably transfer
these loans to the public in a consolidated sterling loan.

5. "Telegram from Michie saying we may expect a remittance.
The NWF will not accept the business we have been hoping
to do." PLB, Sh.-HK., to J. Bell-Irving, Oct. 2, 1886.
Among the many disadvantages of pursuing business through
a network of personal contacts was the atmosphere of
suspicion and frank distrust which often confused judgment
and clouded the record of negotiations. Some of Michie's
remarks in Nei-wu fu correspondence amount to private code
though their intent is obvious: "The Bed Chamber influence
works silently but there are symptoms which are favourable."
Michie learned that other sources were also canvassed by
the Court: "They have been tempted by much lower offers
and the usual delay and reluctance among the higher officials
and the fear of the Censors attacking them for paying a high
rate of interest when lower could be got, has left the
matter open." UC, Tientsin, to J. Keswick, July 20, 1886.

6. Ibid., July 24, 1886.

7. Ibid., Aug. 2, 1886.

8. Ibid., Aug. 3, 1886.

9. Ibid.

10. Ibid.

11. Ibid., Sept. 14, 1886. Keswick explained that "the question
    of ways and means causes me some trouble owing to the
    scarcity of sycee here (Shanghai) and my own engagements
    for kerosene, advances on opium and silk, which can only be
    realized gradually. I see a chance of borrowing a considerable
    sum from Chinese on fixed deposits, which could tide me
    over..." As J.M. & Co. normally paid 5 1/2 per cent to
    5 per cent per annum on fixed deposits, treaty port Chinese
    obviously preferred secure returns to the risks of govern-
    ment business. An example of the manner in which Chinese
    merchants sought the legal shelter of the Treaty Ports was
    an offer made to J. Keswick by the Hun Shan Hong, Shanghai:
    "they wish to know if we will lend our name to advances
    made by them to the Tea dealers up River this coming season,
    so that if they do not fulfill their engagements they can
    apply for redress through us to the British consul at
    Kiukiang and Hankow. If we do this we will require to
    advance on loan to the Hong say Tls. 5 to 10,000 so as to
    qualify us. In return they guarantee to ship their teas,
    75,000 packages...by our River steamers and to give us
    the insurance on same." PLB, Sh.-HK., Sept. 16, 1886
    and Apr. 25, 1885.

12. Payment of the half-million Taels was stalled by the diffi-
    culty of obtaining the necessary sycee in Peking where the
    market had been swept clean by the bank; Shanghai was
    telegraphed but the state of the roads and waterways
    (Sept. 15) between Tientsin and Peking almost prevented
    the arrival of the sycee in time for the half-yearly
    settling day when it was needed by the imperial household.
    Tls. 100,000 was borrowed from the bank in Tientsin and
    shipped by boat while the remainder was rushed by pony from
    Shanghai direct to Peking. Normally the money for advances
    to the department was consigned to Michie's assistant, Chen,
    at Tientsin or Shanghai, then carried under escort to Peking
    where bonds were taken in exchange. Duration of the loans
    was ordinarily twelve months. Such shipments were a great
    risk without a written contract, "A thing impossible to be
    got in Peking." Ibid., Sept. 15, 1886.

13. Ibid., Sept. 16, 1886.

14. Ibid.

15. <u>Ibid.</u>, Sept. 19, 1886.

16. PLB, Sh.-HK., to W. Keswick, Sept. 22, 1886.

17. UC, Tientsin to J. Keswick, Feb. 5, 1887. See also "A Memorial on Imperial Household Finance," <u>North China Herald</u>, June 28, 1887 (September 1887).

18. PLB, Sh.-HK., to J. Macgregor, June 4, 1888.

19. UC, Tientsin, to J. Keswick, May 18, 1888.

20. PLB, Sh.-Tientsin, H.F., to A. Michie, June 14, 1888.

21. <u>Ibid.</u>, July 25, 1888.

22. <u>Ibid.</u>, Aug. 25, 1888.

23. <u>Ibid.</u>, Oct. 12, 1888.

24. <u>Ibid.</u>, Nov. 15, 1888. Michie told Spence that the imperial household "had been ill-used by J.M. & Co.".

25. <u>Ibid.</u>

26. UC, Tientsin, to J. Keswick, Jan. 5, 1889.

27. UC, Sh.-Local, to J.M. & Co., May 17, 1889.

28. The Section of Accounts (November 1889) list the Nei-wu fu loan as: A--Tls. 867,463 (Monthly Interest) Tls. 11,682
                         B--Tls. 630,698 (Monthly Interest) Tls. 9,132
The regularizing of these loans had involved complicated currency and weight problems: "The scales mentioned are not really scales. What I get from the Nei-wu fu was a weight of kuping Tls. 11 which according to the Bonds for Loans A and B should give Kung Fa Tls. 103.40 but actually gives Tls. 103.38. I do not think it necessary to return the weight to the Nei-wu fu and ask for another one with the decided uncertainty of getting it." UC, Tientsin, J. Keswick.

29. PLB, Sh.-Tientsin, H.F. to J. Keswick, May 30, 1889. Fu Ching-tang suggested that the Nei-wu fu might require Tls. 2,000,000 or Tls. 3,000,000.

30. UC, Tientsin, to J. Keswick, Aug. 15, 1889.

31. PLB, Sh.-Tientsin, to D. Spence, June 19, 1889. Macgregor added that the firm would make no fresh loans to the imperial household without an imperial decree; "and seeing the heavy calls upon us for copper finance [reference to Japan] it is scarcely advisable to engage ourselves in anything that cannot be floated."

32. UC, Tientsin, to J. Keswick, July 2, 1889.

33. Ibid. Relations with the Nei-wu fu also allowed the firm
    to keep abreast of their competitors: "Please ask Fu what
    Black Butler is after in Peking. He has been in constant
    communication with Tseng." Even Sir John Walsham's
    representations to the Tsungli Yamen protesting the
    extension of the bonding privilege to China merchant's
    warehouses had been reported to Jardine's from Peking.
    On this matter Keswick commented that "...the British
    Minister comes into conflict at so many points with the
    Chinese that he cannot afford to let cases accumulate,
    to do so surely means defeat, as the Chinese will always
    wait and then under the guise of compromise obtain
    concessions or curtail privileges hitherto regarded as
    the foreigner's rights." These official connections also
    enabled the firm to learn if any of its activities were
    unnecessarily offensive to the Court or other officials,
    as in the case of a "small arms shop" opened by the
    Peking branch in May 1888, selling Armstrong equipment,
    but then closed two months later when Spence learned that
    it was "compromising us with the authorities."

34. PLB, Sh.-HK., to J. Macgregor, July 10, 1889.

35. UC, Tientsin-local, to E. Cousins, Feb. 9, 1889.

36. PLB, Sh.-HK., to J. Macgregor, Sept. 13, 1888.

37. Ibid., July 22, 1888.

38. UC, Tientsin to J. Keswick, Sept. 3, 1888.

39. PLB, Sh.-HK., to J. Macgregor, December 13, 1888.

VII. Railways and Loans

1. UC, Canton-local, 1844.

2. T. De Quincey, China (London, 1857), p. 5; writing during
   the second Anglo-Chinese war.

3. P.H. Kent, Railway Enterprise in China: An Account of its
   Origin and Development (London, 1907), p. 3. Also see
   China Mail, August 11, 1864, p. 127, for Stephenson's own
   words and J.M. & Co. recommendations for a comprehensive
   system of railways centered on Hankow.

4. Ibid., p. 2.

5. Ibid., p. 10 and Accounts, Shanghai, June 1865.

6.   UC, Sh-local, May 16, 1865.

7.   Ibid., May 21, 1865.

8.   Kent, p. 10.

9.   A. Wright, pp. 91-92, and UC, Sh.-local, June 2, 1874.

10. PLB, Sh.-HK., to W. Keswick, June 30, 1876. "The Woosung
    Road is to be opened tonight..."

11. Ibid., July 29, 1876 and Aug. 5, 1876.

12. Ibid., Aug. 12, 1876.

13. F.B. Johnson summarized the agreement: "News from Chefoo.
    The Yunnan business has been arranged. Ichang, Wenchow,
    Wuhu and Pakhoi are opened as ports of Trade. The privilege
    of landing and shipping merchandise and passengers at six
    places along the Yangtze is granted. The upper Yangtze is
    to be navigated as far as Chungking and British officials
    are to be stationed at that place and Yunnan. Indemnity is
    to be paid.." PLB, Sh.-HK., to W. Keswick, Sept. 14, 1876.
    Earlier, he had written "Admiral Ryder has just arrived at
    Woosung but Sir Thomas has made no allusion to coming events
    beyond hinting that many changes will have to be carried
    out by the Chinese Government. War I scarcely believe in."
    Ibid., July 7, 1876.

14. UCB, Sh.-HK., to W. Keswick, Aug. 20, 1876.

15. UC, Sh.-HK., to W. Keswick, July 22, 1876. A "pro-Chinese"
    pamphleteer pointed out that the construction of the railway
    had no treaty sanction and unless repudiated by the British
    government would do great harm. He asked "are Messrs.
    Jardine Matheson and Company more powerful than the Chinese
    Empire, because this railroad of theirs had been made in
    defiance of treaty?" "Justum," England and China (London,
    1887). An American diplomat believed that the manner of
    the railway's building delayed the introduction of railways.
    See C. Holcombe, The Real Chinese Question (London, 1901),
    pp. 10-11. In twelve months the line carried 187,876 people
    and receipts amounted to $42,014. China Mail (HK.),
    Oct. 29, 1877.

16. PLB, Sh.-HK., to W. Keswick, Aug. 25, 1876.

17. PLB, Sh.-HK., to W. Keswick, Sept. 8, 1876.

18. Ibid., Nov. 25, 1876. As late as June 1877 there were reports
    that the Chinese government would extend the line to Foochow.
    China Mail (HK.) June 4, 1877 quoting the Shanghai Shumpo.

The closing of the line caused "great disappointment...as
certainly the credit of China must depend on her taking
some steps to develop the country, and financiers will
not...lend to a nation persistently determined to resist
all changes." <u>Ibid.</u>, September 22, 1877.

19. <u>Ibid.</u>, Sept. 1, 1876.

20. See C.J. Stanley, <u>Late Ch'ing Finance: Hu Kuang-yung as an
    Innovator</u> (Cambridge, Mass. 1961).

21. PLB, Sh.-HK., Nov. 25, 1876. Earlier J. Bell-Irving, Sh.,
    wrote that "should mines be opened and lines laid to them
    in the North we will have a better chance of securing the
    business than if Morrison had not seen Li." <u>Ibid.</u>,
    Sept. 8, 1876.

22. <u>Ibid.</u>, Sept. 28, 1876.

23. <u>Ibid.</u>, See Stanley Spector, <u>Li Hung-chang and the Huai Army</u>
    (Seattle, 1964), p. 298. "The apparently 'reactionary'
    Chinese officials who ultimately bought up and destroyed
    the Woosung Railway were Sheng Hsuan-huai, Chu Chi-chao,
    and Feng Chun-kuang, mainstays of the Li Machine and three
    of the principal economic reformers in China. Despite the
    angry protests of the British and Americans, who accordingly
    wrote highly colored versions of the incident, there can
    be no doubt that the destruction of the Woosung Railway by
    Sheng and his associates was a nationalistic measure, one
    that was aimed at foreigners rather than at foreign innovations."

24. <u>Ibid.</u>, Sept. 9, 1876. "Railway and mining enterprises are
    likely to be encouraged by Li...we should try to obtain the
    position of Bankers and Financial Agents in fact." In
    February 1877, letters and telegrams were exchanged about
    a loan required by the imperial court and assumed to be in
    connection with railways until Michie asked at the Nei-wu fu
    and learned that "Peking Authorities (whom I don't know)
    wanted the money to remove Peh-Tang Cathedral from its
    proximity to the Palace." Jardines' offered to loan
    Tls. 3,000,000 at 8 per cent, if it were sanctioned by
    imperial edict, guaranteed by acceptable securities and
    repaid over five years. The bank, a "German syndicate" and
    an "American syndicate" also tendered. James Keswick tele-
    graphed to William Keswick, then head of Matheson and Co.,
    requesting him "to raise three million Taels with friends
    in London" and Michie was authorized to lend Tls. 400,000
    to Chang Yao, then of the Board of Revenue, "in order to
    help influence a decision on arrangement of the large loan."
    The larger loan was assumed to be for the Taku-Tientsin line.
    Ch'ing officials declined each of these offers. <u>Ibid.</u>,

Jan. 14, 1886, Feb. 5, 1887, Feb. 19, 1887; UC, Tientsin, to J.K., Feb. 19, 1887; PLB, Sh.-Tientsin, Foochow, Hankow, Feb. 20, 27, 1887.

25. In 1883 Li had an interesting talk with Governor Bowen of Hong Kong. He spoke of opposition to railways and the telegraph by "country gentry" and literati. Bowen consoled him by mentioning that English country gentry had also opposed them for a time. China Mail (HK.), Oct. 29, 1883.

26. Kent, p. 28 and Wilson, p. 126 quoting the Peking Gazette.

27. Kent, p. 29. "The Chinese Railway Company met with a cold reception by the Chinese financiers in the north. No subscriptions were received. The capitalists do not trust the officials especially one Chow Fu, [Ch'eng-fu], the Acting Salt Commissioner whose dealings in the Port Arthur contract matter have excited much indignation among Chinese in the North....If railways are to be built in China either foreigners whom these Chinese will trust must be associated in their construction and working, or foreign capital must be solely relied upon." China Mail, May 3, 1887.

28. See the comment by the Chinese Times (Tientsin; edited by Alexander Michie) upon the "great syndicates" and "their mode of exploitation". Quoted in China Mail, Apr. 14, 1887.

29. UC, Tientsin, to J. Keswick, Apr. 18, 1887.

30. UC, Tientsin, to J. Bell-Irving, June 28,, 1887. Heartening confirmation of these hopes had come two months previously when Spence and Liu Ming-chuan signed the Formosa Railroad Contract. "Though cut rather fine owing to competition from our neighbors it still affords us a very fair margin of profit and must count for something in the way of prestige." PLB, Sh.-HK., to J. Bell-Irving, May 13, 1887. Jardine's financed the eighty miles of railroad but had nothing to do with its construction. See Ibid., June 17, 1887.

31. PLB, Sh.-HK., to J. Bell-Irving, July 18, 1887.

32. The firm had recently acted as agents for the Osaka Railroad Company and the Japanese government railways; their Japanese experience seems to have led the firm to misinterpret official decisions in China, to draw close analogies between Meiji programs and Li Hung-chang's slowly coordinated efforts. A large central railroad building program sponsored by the central government was assumed to be inevitable until 1898. UC, Yokohama, to Jardine's, Mar. 15, 1887.

33. UC, Tientsin, to A. Michie, July 21, 1887. To support a
     policy of accepting some small profits while establishing
     its position with the government Keswick pointed to the
     review of accounts in July 1887: Profits were "highly
     satisfactory as a whole..." At Shanghai only the Wharf
     Accounts showed a falling off; Property rents, Cargo
     Boats, the Yuenfah (receiving ship), Commission Accounts,
     Godowns, Insurance and Kerosene Oil Accounts all showed
     gains over the previous year. The Interest Account was
     the largest ever and the Shanghai Credit Balance stood at
     Tls. 302,749 against 1885-1886 Tls. 285,028. In that
     month the Tung Yuen Bank had Tls. 550,000 advanced on
     which the firm charged 7 per cent. All of which provided
     a sound base for agency offers requiring moderate loans
     or joint investment. PLB, Sh.-HK., to J. Bell-Irving,
     July 29, 1887.

34. PLB, Sh.-Tientsin, Hankow, Foochow, to A. Michie, July 28, 1887.

35. Ibid., June 9, 1887. Because of exchange problems, loans
     had to be carefully judged: "We could float the loan in
     China, it is purely a question of naming a rate which
     gives us a profit worth the risks of exchange, etc.,
     and will not be too high to cause the Chinese to go else-
     where. When I say the risks of exchange I mean in case
     we fail to float in China and be obliged to draw."

36. Ibid., Aug. 6, 1887.

37. Ibid.

38. PLB, Sh.-HK., to J. Bell-Irving, Sept. 3, 1887.

39. PLB, Sh.-Tientsin, Hankow, Foochow, to A. Michie,
     Aug. 23, 1887.

40. Ibid., Aug. 20, 1887.

41. PLB, Sh.-HK., to J. Bell-Irving, Sept. 15, 1887.

42. "1887. An Editorial Review of the Events of the Year. The
     Marquis Tseng's paper on 'The sleep and wakening' raised a
     feverish excitement among syndicates and speculators anxious
     to reap the first benefits of the opening up of China.
     Numerous projects for railways, banks, mines, coinage, etc.
     have been launched but very few of them have had any results.
     The greatest of all these schemes was that of an American
     adventurer Count Milkievica, of shady reputation, who came to
     China and dazzled Li Hung-chang with his brilliant project.
     He obtained the promise of vast 'concessions' which were a
     nine day wonder to the world. The bubble soon burst and

the experience will rather have the effect of retarding
than forwarding the development of China." China Mail
(Dec. 31, 1887).

43. Ibid., Aug. 31, 1886.

44. PLB, Sh.-Tientsin, Hankow, Foochow, to A. Michie, July 7, 1886.

45. Ibid., Apr. 15, 1887.

46. Ibid., Apr. 17, 1887.

47. Ibid., Apr. 19, 1887.

48. Ibid., to Gaston Galy, May 12, 1887.

49. PLB, Sh.-HK., to J. Macgregor, Oct. 15, 1889. J. Keswick
     proposed a plan whereby the firm could contribute to the
     financing of Viceroy Chang's scheme by means of the Nei-wu
     fu bonds: "...The Imperial Edict authorizing the Hoppo
     to acknowledge the Bonds...we should get the issue and
     validity of (The Edict) verified by the British Minister.
     With these documents in our possession we could issue a
     Loan in China in silver, Jardine Matheson & Co. being
     issuers and the Security of the Imperial Edict and Bonds
     acknowledged by the Hoppo." The loan would be floated
     in bonds payable to bearer at 6 per cent and he expected
     that the Chinese business community, especially in
     Shanghai, and Hong Kong, would take up the Loan "judging
     by their eagerness to deposit with us at 5 1/2 per cent."
     Nothing came of this plan.

50. See PLB, Sh.-Tientsin, Hankow, Foochow, 1890-1892, for
     J.M. & Co.'s side of the correspondence.

51. Ibid., to E. Cousins, Tientsin, June 4, 1890. Macgregor
     pointed out that the terms "smack very much of terms
     said to have been offered by the Hong Kong and Shanghai
     Bank last year for a gold loan. I should not be at all
     surprised to find that young Li is acting for a Syndicate
     in London with the Bank as the real mover and that the
     American-German Syndicate is put forward as a blind."

52. See PLB, Sh.-Tientsin, H.F., to R. Inglis, Peking,
     June 20, 1890.

53. UC, Tientsin, to J. Keswick, June 28, 1890. "It seems
     that the Peking high officials are not inclined to let
     Li Hung-chang have everything his own way as much as formerly."

54. PLB, Sh.-Tientsin, H.F., to R. Inglis, Peking, June 25, 1890.

55. Ibid., July 3, 1890.

56. Ibid., July 9, 1890.

57. Ibid., July 21, 1890.

58. Ibid., Oct. 27, 1890, Nov. 27, 1890, ff.

59. Ibid., To J. Kup, Peking, Jan. 5, 1891.

60. Ibid., Jan. 28, 1891. "I hope that Mr. Chun will be able
    to get you a copy of Prince Chung's letter through some
    of the latter's servants."

61. Ibid., Feb. 14, 1891. This letter mentions that the firm
    will close the Chinese Times, Tientsin, but continue to
    publish the Shih pao. The latter was controlled by J.M.
    & Co. and Li Hung-chang jointly.

62. Ibid., June 12, 1891, July 23, 1891. "Down to a few days
    ago the house [Russell & Company] had nine establishments
    and during its career it had the most extensive connections
    with the leading financiers all over the world, from
    Barings and Rothschilds to Jamsetjee Jeejeebhoy of Bombay."
    China Mail, June 9, 1891.

63. Ibid., Oct. 8, 1891.

64. One vol. of correspondence: W. Keswick, London, to G.E.
    Montgomery, N.Y., June 15, 1892, Aug. 13, 1892.

65. However, Robert Hart professed belief in China's autonomy.
    He said in 1894: "For China is rich; so much so that if
    her moneyed men only trusted their own government a little
    more, she would undoubtedly soon be in a position to lend
    money to other countries. The curious mistake that
    foreigners have always made with regard to China is to
    imagine that she is in want of extraneous pecuniary
    assistance -- in other words, that she is bordering on
    a state of insolvency. Nothing could be more erroneous.
    Many French, German, and other syndicates have done their
    utmost to induce her to borrow money, but hitherto without
    success...As it has been with loans, so it has been with
    railways. Undoubtedly, China will one day have her railways;
    but though she has for years past been. pestered with offers
    from foreign capitalists to help her start them, so far
    her reply has always been that when the time comes the
    engineers, capital -- all, in fact, that is needful --
    will be found by China -- a strong hint that no foreigners
    need apply." North China Herald, interview with Robert
    Hart aboard S.S. Empress of China, Nagasaki, June 18, 1894.

66. UC, Shanghai, to J. Keswick, July 5, 1890. J. Macgregor
     referred to the great advantage of having a single, central
     authority promoting economic development.

67. PLB, Sh.-HK., to J. Keswick, June 10, 1894. Li Hung-chang
     had Tls. 600,000 invested with the firm on that date.

68. Ibid., June 20, 1894.

69. "The London market had great faith in an Imperial Edict
     with its promise upon the revenues of the maritime customs."
     Ibid., July 27, 1894.

70. Ibid., July 27, 1894. "To avoid competition, consult with
     the Bank, (and) try to get the loan firm in hand and then
     consult together to see what can best be done."

71. UC, Tientsin, to J. Macewen, Aug. 18, 1894. "Cousins
     will endeavor to get Sheng Taotai to put the business in
     our way. 6 per cent is our rate, subject to modification."

72. Ibid., telegrams from J. Keswick, Oct. 20, 1894. There
     were several references to German influence: "The C.M.
     outbid the Hongkew Wharf Co. for the dock property. I
     fancy the Germans must be behind them." Cousins protested
     that Sheng's offer to give the loan to Jardine's had been
     no more than a bribe but Keswick was inclined to assume
     that the offer was genuine since Tientsin did not always
     know what Peking intended: "...of course everybody is
     down on Sheng but I don't think he is as bad as he is
     pointed out or at least any worse than others of his class."

73. PLB, Sh.-HK., to J. Keswick, Nov. 22, 1894.

74. PLB, Sh.-HK., to J. Keswick, Mar. 22, 1895. "Mr. Consul
     Jamisson read me a letter he had received from M. O'Conor
     (British Minister in Peking) in which our name was
     mentioned and urging activity of British vs. German
     interests." A similar plea had been made to the Hong Kong
     and Shanghai Bank.

75. UC, Sh.-Tientsin, to J. Macewen, Mar. 28, 1895. They
     added, however, that silver and gold loans recently made
     to China by the bank had been improving on the London
     market because of rumors that the war would soon end and
     renewed confidence in China's ability to meet debts
     incurred. The government had attempted to float internal
     loans during the first months of the war but could not
     command the confidence of potential investors. The treaty
     port commercial class resisted official pressures,
     therefore "China was compelled to seek external credits

for the prosecution of the war." The Hong Kong Bank
loans (£ 1,635,000 at seven per cent and £ 5,000,000
at six per cent) were used to meet war costs and to
buy more arms (including a £ 100,000 contract for
Krupp cannon through Jardines). Keswick wrote that
Hart was "the moving spirit behind the bank loans," for
which agreements had been signed in London by the
Chinese Minister. See A.G. Coons, The Foreign Public
Debt of China (London, 1930), p. 5. Also UC, Sh.-
to H. Smith, June 3, 1894.

76. PLB, Sh.-HK., to J. Keswick, Mar. 24, 1895. See also
Timothy Richard, Forty-Five Years in China (New York,
1916), pp. 232-241. Richard told Chang "that God
demanded reform on the part of China, and that if
she neglected it, God would appoint some other nation
to reform her..." Richard was not a "close friend"
of the viceroy.

77. Ibid., Apr. 13, 1895.

78. Ibid. "J.M. To Build Railway -- The 'Bangkok Times,'
on the authority of a correspondent in China, says
that J.M. & Co. have obtained a confession from the
Chinese Govereent for the construction of a railway
from Peking to Chinkiang, and the Imperial edict has
already been signed. No confirmation of the rumor is
obtainable in Hong Kong but we have reason to believe
that there is some truth in it. -- Local and General."
China Mail, Aug. 26, 1895.

79. PLB, Sh.-HK. to J. Keswick, Apr. 24, 1895.

80. Ibid.

81. Ibid. See also China Mail, Mar. 17, 1896 on the Hong
Kong and Shanghai Bank securing of "the Great Loan,"
Tls. 100,000,000 (£ 16,000,000) at five per cent in
in gold.

82. Ibid., Apr. 28, 1895.

83. Ibid., Apr. 26, 1895.

84. UC, HK., to J. Keswick, May 17, 1895.

85. UC, Sh.-HK., press copy to HK. & Sh. Banking Corp.,
Aug. 14, 1895.

86. See China Mail, July 8, 1898.

Conclusion

1. I base the Tls. 5,000,000 investment estimate on Accounts, Ledgers and Journals, HK., 1885, and on a rough calculation of the capital absorbed by the firm's establishments in China and Hong Kong.

2. Pelcovitz, p. 2.

3. Ibid., p. 157.

4. 270. Nicholas Kaldor, Essays on Economic Stability and Growth (London, Duckworth, 1960), p. 235.

5. In 1881 W. Keswick said in a public speech: "I believe that the intercourse of the Chinese with European enterprise has had its effects and before long there will be powerful converts in China to the importance of following Western ideas..." He also spoke of "the promotion of wealth, not to us alone, but to the millions of China." China Mail (HK.), May 16, 1881.

6. See Mao Tse-tung, The Chinese Revolution and the Chinese Communist Party, Selected Works, Vol. 3 (New York,,1955), pp. 78-79 and Hu Sheng, Imperialism and Chinese Politics (Peking, 1955), p. 111 for Chinese Marxist views on Western economic pressure.

BIBLIOGRAPHY

Archives of Jardine, Matheson and Company. Deposited at Cambridge
University Library, Cambridge, England. The following
sections were consulted:

Accounts, Section of

    Journals: 1844, 1845, 1863-1864, 1867-1868, 1875-1876,
        1878, 1885-1886, 1887.

    Ledgers: 1844-1845, 1846-1847, 1853-1854, 1863-1864,
        1874-1878 (Japan), 1874-1875, 1880, 1881-
        1882, 1884.

Correspondence, Unbound: Incoming Correspondence

    London (1842-1898), Calcutta (1842-1893), Bombay
      (1845-1850)

    Local: Peking (1860-1901)
             Port Arthur (1886-1901)
             Shanghai (1844-1891)
             Hong Kong (1850-1895)
             Tientsin (1860-1901)
             Foochow & River Min (1846-1890)
             Formosa (1855-1901)

    Private Letters:

             London (1840-1882)
             Shanghai (1844-1888)
             Foochow & River Min (1854-1880)

Letter Books

    India: from Hong Kong, 1844-1883, 10 vols.
    Europe: from Hong Kong, 1844-1898, 15 vols.
    Coast: selected vols. from Hong Kong, 1842-1883
    Miscellaneous: general series from Shanghai, May 1858,
            then selected vols. to August 1885
    Hong Kong to London (Piece Goods), 1868-1883, 2 vols.
    Private: Alexander Matheson, August 1841-January 1846
          Hong Kong to India, 1846-1885, 10 vols.

Press Copy Letter Books

    Hong Kong to Coast: selected, 1882-1896, 5 vols.
    Hong Kong Banking and Financial: (Book Offfice),
        1887-1895, 2 vols.
    China Sugar Refinery, 1883-1913, 3 vols.
    Korea: June 1883-August 1884, 1 vol.
    Private: Shanghai to Hong Kong, May 1876-May 1895,
        14 vols.
    Indo-China S.N. Co., 1886-1889, 1 vol.
    London and Pacific Petroleum Co., Ltd., 1890-1894,
        1 vol.

Telegram Books

    16 vols., 1875-1896
    2 bound vols. of semi-official correspondence, 1890-1908

Occasional Market Reports, 1842-1895

One box of Manifests

Occasional Cash Books, Shanghai

Arnold, J., Commerical Handbook of China
    (Washington, 1919).

Bales, W.L., Tso Tsung-t'ang: Soldier and Statesman of Old China
    (Shanghai, 1937).

Beal, E.G., Jr., The Origin of Likin, 1853-1864 (Cambridge, Mass.,
    1958).

Bland, J.O.P., Li Hung-chang (New York, 1917).

------   China Under the Empress Dowager (London, 1910).

BPP: British Parliamentary Papers

    Papers Relating to the Opium Trade in China, 1842-1856
    Session, February 1857, Vol. 43.

Report from the Select Committee of the Commons on Commercial Relations with China, 1847 Session, Jan. 19-July 23, 1847.

Correspondence Relating to the Earl of Elgin's Special Mission to China and Japan, 1857-1859, 1859, Vol. 33.

Correspondence Respecting Affairs in China, Oct. 1859 to Jan. 1861, 1861, Vol. 66.

Correspondence Respecting the Opening of the Yangtze to Foreign Trade, 1861, Vol. 66.

Correspondence Respecting the Chefoo Agreement, 1880, Vol. 78 and 1882, Vol. 80.

Brown, H., Parry's of Madras (London, 1954).

Cairncross, A.K., Home and Foreign Investment, 1870-1913 (Cambridge, England, 1953).

Carlson, Ellsworth, The Kaiping Mines, 1877-1912 (Cambridge, Mass., 1957).

Celestial Empire, The (June-July 1877).

Chang Chih-tung, "China's Only Hope," tr. Samuel I. Woodbridge (New York, 1900).

Chi Ch'ao-ting, "Key Economic Areas in Chinese History, As Revealed in the Development of Public Works for Water-Control" (London: Institute of Pacific Relations, 1936).

China, Imperial Maritime Customs, see IMC.

China Mail, The (July 1873-October 1900).

China Overland Trade Report (Hong Kong, Mar. 1, 1879).

China Review, The (1878-1882).

China, The Maritime Customs, Treaties, Conventions, etc. between China and Foreign States. Vol. 1., (Shanghai, 1917).

Chinese Repository, The (1844-1849).

Clapham, J.H., An Economic History of Modern Britain, 3 vols. (Cambridge, England, 1926-1938).

Collins, W.F., Mineral Enterprise in China (Tientsin, 1922).

Colquhoun, A.R., The Opening of China: Six Letters to The Times of London (August 1884).

Commercial Reports of Her Majesty's Consuls in China (London, 1869 through 1884). Foreign Office, Consular Trade Reports.

Cooke, G.W., China (London: Routledge and Company, 1858).

Coons, A.G., The Foreign Public Debt of China (Philadelphia, 1930).

Costin, W.C., Great Britain and China, 1833-1860 (Oxford, 1937).

Couling, S., ed., Encyclopedia Sinica, 2 vols. (Shanghai, 1937).

DeQuincey, T., China (London, 1857). Pamphlet.

Duckerts, Jules, La Chine en 1889. Rapport de la Mission Commerciale de Jules Duckerts, Consul General, Chargé d'affaires de Belgique (Verviers, 1901).

Duhalde, Pere, The General History of China (London, 1741).

Economic Development and Cultural Change (October 1960).

Economic History Review, The, ed. M.M. Postan and J.H. Habakkuk, 2nd series, Vol. 6, Nos. 1, 2, 3 (1953-1954).

Endacott, G.B., The History of Hong Kong (Oxford, 1958).

Fairbank, John K., Trade and Diplomacy on the China Coast: The Opening of the Treaty Ports, 1842-1854, 2 vols. (Cambridge, Mass., 1953).

------, ed., Chinese Thought and Institutions (Chicago, 1957).

------, Alexander Eckstein and L.S. Yang, "Economic Change in Early Modern China: An Analytic Framework," Economic Development and Cultural Change (October 1960).

Fei Hsiao-tung, China's Gentry: Essays in Rural-Urban Relations (Chicago, 1952).

Feuerwerker, A., China's Early Industrialization (Cambridge, Mass., 1958).

Fong, H.D. "Cotton Industry and Trade in China," The Chinese Social-Political Science Review 16:392 (1932-1933).

Forbes, F.E., Five Years in China (London, 1848).

Fortune, R., Three Years Wanderings in the Northern Provinces of China, Including a Visit to the Tea, Silk & Cotton Countries (London, 1847).

------A Journey to the Tea Countries of China (London, 1852).

------Two Visits to the Tea Countries of China. 2 vols. (London, 1853).

------A Residence Among the Chinese: Inland, on the Coast and at Sea. Being a narrative of scenes and adventures during a third visit to China from 1853 to 1856. (London, 1857).

------Journey to China and Japan (London, 1863).

Gilbert, R., The Unequal Treaties (London, 1929).

Gorst, H.E., History of China, Political, Commercial and Social (London, 1899).

Gras, N.S.B., "Business History," in Economic History Review, Vol. 4, No. 4.

Greenberg, Michael, British Trade and the Opening of China, 1800-1942 (Cambridge, England, 1951).

Hail, W.J., Tseng Kuo-fan and the Taiping Rebellion (New Haven, 1927).

Hart, Robert, These From the Land of Sinim: Essays on the Chinese Question (London, 1903).

Hinton, H.C., The Grain Tribute System of China, 1845-1911. (Chinese Economic and Political Studies; Cambridge, Mass., 1956).

Ho Ping-ti, Studies on the Population of China, 1368-1953 (Cambridge, Mass., 1959).

------, "The Salt Merchants of Yang-chou: A Study of Commercial Capitalism in 18th Century China," Harvard Journal of Asiatic Studies, 17. 1-2:130-168.

Ho, Ping-yin, The Foreign Trade of China (Shanghai, 1935).

Holcombe, C., The Real Chinese Question (London, 1901).

Hong Kong Register, The (March 1858).

Hsu, I.C.Y., China's Entrance into the Family of Nations: The Diplomatic Phase, 1858-1880 (Cambridge, Mass., 1960).

Hummel, A.W., ed., Eminent Chinese of the Ch'ing Period, 1644-1912, 2 vols. (Washington, D.C., 1943-1944).

IMC: China, Imperial Maritime Customs

Reports on Trade at the Treaty Ports, annually, 1865-1875 (Shanghai: Inspectorate General of Customs).

Returns of Trade at the Treaty Ports of China, 1870-1881.

Returns of Trade at the Treaty Ports and Trade Reports, 1882-1912.

Jernigan, T.R., China in Law and Commerce (New York, 1905).

"Justum," England and China (London, 1887).

Kent, P.H., Railway Enterprise in China: An Account of Its Origin and Development (London, 1907).

Ketels, M., Le Role du Compradore dans les Relations Commerciales en Chine. (Chine et Belgique: Juilliet, 1906). pp. 99-102.

Kiernan, E.V.G., British Diplomacy in China, 1880-1885 (Cambridge, England, 1939).

King, P., In the Chinese Customs Service, A Personal Record of Forty-Seven Years (London, 1924, Rev. ed., 1930).

Knollys, H., English Life in China (London, 1885).

Krausse, A., China in Decay (London, 1900).

Larson, H.M., Guide to Business History. (Cambridge, Mass., 1948).

Levy, M.J., and Shih Kuo-ling. The Rise of The Modern Chinese Business Class. (New York, 1949).

Liu, K.C., Anglo-American Steamship Rivalry in China, 1862-1874 (Cambridge, Mass., 1962).

Lockwood, W.W., The Economic Development of Japan: Growth and Structural Change, 1868-1938 (Princeton, 1954).

Lubbock, A.B., The Opium Clippers (Boston, 1933).

Matheson, J., Present Position and Prospects of British Trade with China (London, 1836).

Martin, R.M., China: Political, Commercial and Social. 2 vols. (London, 1847).

Mayers, W.F., The Chinese Government (Shanghai, 1897).

------,St. Charles King and N.B. Dennys, eds., Treaty Ports of China and Japan (London and Hong Kong, 1867).

Meadows, T.T., The Chinese and Their Rebellions (London, 1856).

Michie, A., The Englishman in China During the Victorian Era. 2 vols. (London, 1900).

Milburn, W., Oriental Commerce (London, 1825).

Morse, H.B., The Guilds of China (London, 1909).

------The International Relations of the Chinese Empire. 3 vols. (London, 1910-1918).

------Trade and Administration of the Chinese Empire (Shanghai, 1913).

------The Trade and Administration of China (London, 1921; Rev. ed., Shanghai, 1913).

Murphey, R., Shanghai, Key to Modern China (Cambridge, Mass., 1953).

North China Herald and Supreme Court Consular Gazette, 1866, 1868, 1871, 1873.

North China Herald Retrospect of Political and Commercial Affairs in China, 1868-1872.

Osborn, S., The Past and Future of British Relations in China (London, 1860).

Owen, D.E., Imperialism and Nationalism in the Far East (London, 1929).

------British Opium Policy in China and India (New Haven and London, 1934).

Pelcovitz, N.A., Old China Hands and the Foreign Office (New York, 1948).

Power, W.T., Recollections of Three Years Residence in China (London, 1853).

Remer, C.F., The Foreign Trade of China (Shanghai, 1926).

Richard, Timothy, Forty-Five Years in China (New York, 1916).

Richthoffen, Baron von., Letters, 1870-1872 (Shanghai, 1903).

Sargent, A.J., Anglo-Chinese Commerce and Diplomacy (Oxford, 1907).
Scarth, J., Twelve Years in China: The People, the Rebels and the Mandarins. By a British Resident (Edinburgh, 1860).

See Chong-su, The Foreign Trade of China (New York, 1919).

Spector, Stanley, Li Hung-chang and the Huai Army (Seattle, 1964).

Stanley, C.J., "Chinese Finance from 1852 to 1907," Papers on China, 3:1-23 (Harvard University, East Asian Research Center, 1949).

------Late Ch'ing Finance: Hu Kuang-yung as an Innovator (Cambridge, Mass., 1961).

Supreme Court and Consular Gazette and Law Reporter, for Her Britannic Majesty's Supreme Court and Provincial Courts and the Consular Courts of China and Japan (Shanghai, 1867-1869).

Teng, Ssu-yü, New Light on the History of the Taiping Rebellion (Cambridge, Mass., 1950).

------, and John K. Fairbank, China's Response to the West: A Documentary Survey, 1839-1923 (Cambridge, Mass., 1954).

Torr, D., ed., "Marx on China, 1853-1860," Articles from the New York Daily Tribune (London, 1951).

Wagel, G.R., Finance in China (Shanghai, 1914).

Westminster Review, The (October 1868, January 1870).

Willoughby, W.W., Foreign Rights and Interest in China. 2 vols. (Baltimore, 1927).

Wilson, J.H., China: Travels and Investigations in the Middle Kingdom (New York, 1888).

Wright, A., Twentieth Century Impressions of Hong Kong, Shanghai, and Other Treaty Ports of China (London, 1908).

Wright, M.C., The Last Strand of Chinese Conservatism: The T'ung-Chih Restoration, 1863-1874 (Stanford, 1957).

Wright, S.F., China's Struggle for Tariff Autonomy 1843-1938 (Shanghai, 1938).

------, Hart and the Chinese Customs (Belfast, 1950).

Yang, Tuan-liu and H.B. Hau, Statistics of China's Foreign Trade During the Last Sixty-Five Years (Nanking, 1931).

Yung, W., My Life in China and America (New York, 1909).

INDEX

HARVARD EAST ASIAN MONOGRAPHS, 26